Gospel Fueled Joy
By Maranatha Baptist University
Cover Design by Jonathan Williquette

Published by Maranatha Baptist University
745 West Main St.
Watertown, WI 53094
www.mbu.edu

First Edition, 2019
Manufactured in the United States of America

Preface

Chapel is an integral part of Maranatha discipleship. For 50 years the chapel hour has been used by God to bind the Maranatha family together as we unite in worship around the Word of God. We believe God's Word is alive and powerful; it is the sword used by the Holy Spirit to convict of sin, to comfort the brokenhearted, to encourage the fallen, to call believers to service, and to lead them in the winding paths of life. Only the Word of God will change hearts.

Maranatha's mission goes beyond dispensing information and conferring degrees. Students are challenged to live for Christ and to be to the praise of His glory, by walking in daily submission to God's will. Gathering together for daily chapel during one of the most valuable hours of the educational day is a testimony to our corporate humility. We are completely dependent on God, individually for His guidance, and institutionally for the future of Maranatha Baptist University.

From my first day as Maranatha's president, I have affirmed our commitment to ministry being the center of our identity. In my first meeting with alumni in 2010, I reminded them that our heritage is one of ministry training and that liberal arts education has changed the entire direction of many institutions. Ivy League schools, which now have no semblance of religious affection, were founded to train ministers of the gospel; many schools have lost their way over the centuries and in recent decades. Chapel helps keep our mission in focus.

Maranatha teaches and encourages expository preaching. However, since expository, verse-by-verse book studies are not possible with guest speakers, this year the Bible faculty undertook the task of preaching through the books of Philippians and Titus over the course of two semesters. Our passion as a faculty is to communicate the truth of Scripture by focusing on the text, explaining the meaning, and applying the truth to the lives of the listeners.

The sermons in this volume were a blessing to the Maranatha family. It is our hope and prayer that they may be of help to other students, Sunday school teachers, Bible study groups, and churches.

His for Service,

Marty Marriott

Contributors

Marty Marriott (DD) became the President of Maranatha Baptist University in 2009. He earned two bachelors and two masters degrees and received a Doctor of Divinity from MBU in 2007. He began his ministry as a church planter and served in the pastorate for thirty years. He enjoys reading, preaching, and spending time with family.

Mark Herbster (MDiv) is the Dean of the College of Bible and Church Ministries and Maranatha Baptist Seminary and teaches pastoral theology and homiletics. He enjoys travelling, preaching, and sports.

Bryan Brock (DMin, Expository Preaching) teaches homiletics, apologetics, doctrine and Bible courses. He loves investing in people in the three spheres of his life: family, church ministry, and the university.

Andrew Hudson (PhD, New Testament) teaches Greek and New Testament. He enjoys college sports and traveling with his family to historically significant sights.

Steve Love (DMin) teaches missions and cross-cultural classes in the college. He enjoys interim pastoral work, restoring antique cars, and working in his wood shop.

Preston Mayes (PhD, Old Testament) teaches Old Testament, Hebrew, and Greek. He enjoys spending time with his family, bowling, and water skiing.

Bruce Meyer (DMin, Biblical Counseling) teaches doctrine, theology, Bible, and biblical counseling for the university in both the college and seminary. He enjoys all things Sabercat, reading, and woodworking.

Fred Moritz (DMin) teaches Systematic Theology, Baptist polity, and Theological Issues in Missions in the seminary. He boldly cheers for Alabama Crimson Tide football and the Minnesota Vikings.

Larry Oats (PhD, Systematic Theology) teaches theology and related subjects in the college and seminary. He enjoys writing and traveling with his wife to visit his twelve grandchildren.

David Saxon (PhD, Church History) teaches church history, Baptist history, Bible, and theology. He loves expository preaching and enjoys participating in chapel book series.

Contents

Created, Contagious Joy

Philippians 1:1-8 | Mark Herbster

[1]Paul and Timotheus, the servants of Jesus Christ, to all the saints in Christ Jesus which are at Philippi, with the bishops and deacons: [2]Grace be unto you, and peace, from God our Father, and from the Lord Jesus Christ.[3]I thank my God upon every remembrance of you, [4]Always in every prayer of mine for you all making request with joy, [5]For your fellowship in the gospel from the first day until now; [6]Being confident of this very thing, that he which hath begun a good work in you will perform it until the day of Jesus Christ: [7]Even as it is meet for me to think this of you all, because I have you in my heart; inasmuch as both in my bonds, and in the defence and confirmation of the gospel, ye all are partakers of my grace. [8]For God is my record, how greatly I long after you all in the bowels of Jesus Christ.

Greetings to the Philippian Church
v. 1 Paul and Timothy, the servants of Jesus Christ.

Notice that Paul does not begin his epistle as he often does: "Paul, an apostle of Jesus Christ." He does not remind them of his apostolic leadership, most likely because he was sending a friendly letter. He didn't want to lift himself above the church.

He says in verse 1, "To all the saints which are at Philippi, with the bishops and deacons." He calls himself simply a servant and saint of God. And isn't that what we all are? Servants. He mentions Timothy, who is not an apostle, in the same greeting: Paul and Timothy. He doesn't say, "I am an apostle, and Timothy is my disciple." Timothy was most likely the one who helped Paul write his letter to the Philippians while Paul was in prison in Rome. Timothy became kind of the secretary for the Apostle Paul, and we know that Paul had a love for him and he says that they are both servants. Philippians chapter 2 reminds us that Jesus Himself took on the form of a servant. Servanthood is a theme throughout the book.

Paul is literally calling himself a slave, "to all the saints in Christ Jesus which are in Philippi, with the bishops and deacons." As Baptists we believe in two offices in the church: pastor and deacon. And we know that the word "bishop" here literally means "overseer," which is emphasizing a different aspect of the same office as "pastor" and "elder" in the New

Testament. They are the leaders, and the question is, why did he mention the leaders?

We can speculate a little bit on this: there must have been something going on in the leadership, perhaps some selfishness and division, because we see that theme throughout the book. He mentions the leadership, perhaps so they know that his letter is not just for the congregation at large, but for them as well. Selfishness, which is addressed in chapter 2, may have been a problem for the leaders of the church as well as the people in the congregation.

Verse 2 is the common greeting: "Grace be unto you, and peace, from God our Father, and from the Lord Jesus Christ." Paul then shares a prayer of thanksgiving and remembrance – a prayer that brings great joy to his heart, in verses 3-8.

The Setting

The city of Philippi was named after Philip II of Macedon, who was the father of Alexander the Great. Most likely Philip II travelled to this area of Macedonia to mine gold in the surrounding mountains. He conquered the city and named it after himself and Philippi remained the name of the city through the Roman conquest and continued even until the time of Paul. Many significant historic events happened in the city of Philippi.

Philippi was referred to in other places in the NT, for example, 2 Cor. 8. The people of Philippi were suffering under Roman rule at this time in history even as Paul was suffering in Rome. In 2 Corinthians 8:1 Paul describes this church in this way: "Moreover, brethren, we do you to wit of the grace of God bestowed on the churches of Macedonia [obviously including—maybe even exclusively—the city of Philippi]." Notice that at the time of his writing, the church was in "a great trial of affliction" and yet they had an "abundance" of joy in their "deep poverty." You see, your joy is not dependent on your circumstances. Your joy is dependent on the gospel. Gospel-fueled joy!

So even this church was struggling with responding in joy. They had deep poverty and yet joy in their deep poverty. We know that this was the only church, according to Philippians 4, that ministered to Paul in an actual financial way by giving him gifts early on and also sending gifts by

Epaphroditus. Though they were in deep poverty, though they had great suffering, they had joy in the gospel. So much so that they supported Paul the missionary, the evangelist, and apostle.

So, clearly, Paul is talking about the church of Philippi in 2 Cor. 8:1. Notice verses 3-5: "For to their power, I bear record, yea, and beyond their power they were willing of themselves, praying us with much entreaty that we would receive the gift, and take upon us the fellowship of the ministering to the saints. And this they did, not as we hoped, but first gave their own selves to the Lord, and unto us by the will of God."

Now back to Philippians 1. This church ministered to Paul in a very special way; Paul had a special relationship with them. The situation of the church was pain, suffering and poverty. The situation for Paul dire. At the time he wrote this book of Philippians he was in prison in Rome, most likely in some sort of house arrest. Four times in chapter 1 he says he is "in bonds." This is amazing! Here is a man suffering in chains in prison, and he is writing to a suffering church, and the theme is gospel-fueled joy! How can you have joy in pain and suffering? Only when your life is built upon something strong and sure: the foundation of the gospel of Jesus Christ.

Several commentators comment on this theme of joy. "Joy is the keynote of this epistle. The sum of this epistle is 'I rejoice; you rejoice,'" says one.[1] Another says, "Divine joy is the theme of Philippians. The Greek word for *joy* in both its noun and verb forms occur over a dozen times in its four chapters."[2] And another commentator gives this insight: "Joy is the music that runs through this epistle, the sunshine that spreads over all of it. The whole epistle radiates joy and happiness."[3]

---

[1] Vincent, M. R., *Word Studies in the New Testament* vol.3 (New York: Charles Scribner's Sons, 1887), 416.

[2] MacArthur, J. F., Jr., *Philippians* (Chicago: Moody Press. 2001), pg. 1.

[3] Quoting Lenski, MacArthur, J. F., Jr., *Philippians* (Chicago: Moody Press. 2001), pg. 3.

Here is the main idea for this opening passage: *Friendship and fellowship in the gospel creates a contagious joy in the life of a believer.* That statement makes me think of the excitement and the enthusiasm that I get anytime that I can be with the most loved people in my life: my family. Every year my brothers and their families, my family, and my parents get together for the "Herbster Family Vacation." And it brings us all great joy. As a matter of fact, it kind of keeps me going most of the year as I look forward to it. We schedule those vacations a year or two in advance, and just thinking about it and knowing it is coming, knowing the laughter and tears that we will share, the time with the Lord that we will share, brings a sense of satisfaction and joy to my heart through all the difficulties and trials of life. Thinking about that fellowship and friendship brings joy. And I think, in a sense, that is exactly what is happening here in this text. Paul is in prison; he is in chains; he is in bonds; he is suffering. But the very thought of his fellowship and friendship with these people brings to him great joy. How can we have this contagious joy? *We can have this joy as we relate to other people in these five ways:*

We must be thankful for fellow-saints.
v. 3 *I thank my God upon every remembrance of you*

Paul says he was thankful for them. Notice that in each of these verses there is a phrase like "unto you" (v. 2), "of you" (v. 3), "for you" (v. 4), "in you" (v.6), "of you" (v. 7), "long after you" (v. 8). And the point is, you can't have this kind of contagious joy in fellowship and friendship if your eyes are all on you! You must stop thinking about yourself and start focusing on others. And the first thing that Paul tells the church at Philippi is, *"I thank my God upon every remembrance of you."* He was thankful for this church, and he expressed it to them. This is the first activity that generates joy as we recollect, and we remember different people. It brings great joy to our hearts.

We must be praying for fellow-saints.
v. 4 *Always in every prayer of mine for you all*

Not only is Paul thankful for these saints, but secondly, he is praying for them. This prayer was motivated by his friendship and his fellowship. Question: are you praying for other students? Are you praying for your friends? Are you praying for your local church? As you think about and pray for others, you begin to experience great joy!

We must be optimistic for fellow-saints.
v. 6 *Being confident of this very thing*

This optimism is not a psychological, self-help idea. This is an optimism which is built upon the serious and profound theological truth that Jesus Christ, who started our salvation, is the One who works in our hearts, the One who draws us to faith; He is the One who reconciles us and redeems us and is sanctifying us and justifies us, and eventually He will complete it! That is something that we can be optimistic about; someday we will be glorified, and we will be with God! He will complete that which He starts. One person said it this way: "God is not like men. Men conduct experiments, but God carries out a plan. God never does anything in half[4]." And so, we know that we can be optimistic about other people. Someone may be struggling; someone may even be a rebel and be backslidden, but if they are a genuine believer, we can have confidence that God is working, right? And this is the kind of spirit we should have. It releases joy, and it is contagious.

We must be empathetic towards fellow-saints.
v. 7 *Even as it is meet for me to think this of you all because I have you in my heart;*

Verse 7, "Even as it is meet for me to think this of you" [the idea is 'feeling this for you.' It is the attitude of our mind which generates that emotion of empathy—going along with other people in their sorrows and sadness], because I have you in my heart." You can't read this without sensing the kind of joy Paul had in the friendship and fellowship with these believers! Why are we so eager to get away from church? Why aren't we hanging out with brothers and sisters even more? Maybe we are so busy that we aren't even receiving this kind of joy from God's people. Friendship and fellowship with God's people creates a contagious joy.

We must be affectionate towards fellow-saints.
v. 8 *For God is my record, how greatly I long after you all in the bowels of Jesus Christ.*

---

[4] Quoting William Hendriksen, MacArthur, J. F., Jr., *Philippians* (Chicago: Moody Press. 2001), pg. 29.

We must have an affection for others. This comes from the word "bowels." It may sound strange, but the idea is the "affections," the loving affection he had for his people. Almost every occurrence of this word for "bowels" refers to the affection of the heart. John 13:35 says, "By this shall all men know that ye are my disciples: if ye have love one to another."

And so, as we start on this "Gospel-fueled Joy" theme, we must remember that this kind of joy comes as we fellowship in the gospel. Remember this also: you are very blessed to be around this number of believers. You are very blessed to be able to go out every weekend and be around God's people in local churches. That kind of friendship and fellowship is rare. And it should create in you a great joy as you are thankful, as you are praying, as you're optimistic and empathetic and affectionate. In these kinds of ways, it will generate in you real joy. It is created and is contagious through friendship and fellowship. And this is the fellowship of the gospel, which motivates this satisfaction in Jesus Christ alone. By God's grace, even today you will get great joy out of the friendship and fellowship that you have even here at MBU.

God's Good Work in Us

Philippians 1:9-11 | Dr. David Saxon

⁹ And this I pray, that your love may abound yet more and more in knowledge and in all judgment; ¹⁰ That ye may approve things that are excellent; that ye may be sincere and without offence till the day of Christ. ¹¹ Being filled with the fruits of righteousness, which are by Jesus Christ, unto the glory and praise of God.

Introduction

How's your joy? To measure joy, I suppose we need to know what it is. In our examination we need to avoid two wrong perceptions. On the one hand, some people are naturally sanguine. They wake up whistling a happy tune (sometimes to the annoyance of those around them), and they giggle a lot. That may or may not have any relation to biblical joy. On the other hand, some people assure us that they have biblical joy—not the flighty emotional stuff, but the real thing—but they are continually glum, smile only when extremely provoked, and generally seem to be having a miserable time of it. While we grant that biblical joy can coexist with deep sorrow, it is unlikely that it can coexist with pessimism. Those with biblical joy will not be "nattering nabobs of negativity."

Definition of Joy

So, what is biblical joy? Consider the following definition:

> *Biblical joy is Spirit-enabled contentment with God and His will that restrains from sinful responses and is the mainspring of our satisfaction and happiness.*

Are you content with God and His will? Are you responding patiently to the pressures and problems of life? Are you satisfied with what God has provided for you and, when appropriate, are you happy? These are more adequate measures of biblical joy, as the Scriptures present it.

How does one get such joy? Consider an analogy. Suppose a person wanted to be an athlete simply because he has seen victory celebrations in the end zone after a touchdown in football, and he thinks it would be great to experience that "joy." If his sole purpose were this thrilling but brief emotion, how committed would he be during the long, difficult practices, the recovery from injuries, and the inevitable defeats and struggles that serious athletes must endure? The pursuit of emotional experiences will not sustain effort. A real athlete aims at improvement, competitiveness, and ultimately mastery of his sport. Victories and the emotional satisfactions that come with them are byproducts of this more fundamental pursuit. One could say he is pursuing joy, but he is not caught up in momentary happiness but rather his sights are set higher. He wants the long-term joy of being an accomplished athlete. Obviously, the same dynamic would apply to a musician or a scholar pursuing mastery of his craft. Joy is the goal, in a sense, but the joy is not a fruit of the pursuit but part and parcel of the pursuit. The real athlete doesn't get joy only *from* sports; he gets joy *in* sports.

The Christian life has a similar dynamic at work. Paul does not urge the Philippians to focus on their own happiness. He urges them to focus on Christ and the gospel. But pursuing Christ and the gospel inevitably involves real, biblical joy, or, as this series is subtitled, gospel-fueled joy.

Our text, 1:9-11, is one of the paragraphs in Philippians that does not explicitly mention joy. This paragraph is a prayer Paul is offering for the Philippians. He doesn't pray that they will have joy; he prays that they will become mature, Christ-empowered, God-glorifying Christians.

As exposited in the previous section, we saw in verse 6 that Paul is confident that the Philippians are true believers; therefore, God is going to complete the work He began in them, and He is going to do so until Christ returns. The fact that God is going to accomplish this work in the life of each Philippian believer does not make Paul passive; rather, it drives him to his knees. A proper confidence in God's sovereignty and plan always leads to prayer that God will do His work. It does not lead to apathy or inactivity, but to faith.

Verses 9-11 contain a powerful wish-prayer of Paul for the Philippians. Consider the seven aspects of this prayer.

Overflowing Love
v. 9a "And this I say, that your love may abound yet more and more …"

Paul first prays that the Philippians' love may overflow. Interestingly, Paul mentions "love" only four times in Philippians, but it is the first request he makes for them. In chapter four we will discover that one of Paul's purposes in writing the letter is to help the Philippians resolve issues that are separating them, so it is not surprising that he would emphasize love.

The word *abound* means to overflow. In August 2018, just weeks before this sermon was preached, the Rock River, which flows through Watertown, Wisconsin, overflowed. It surpassed its natural boundaries, thus flooding a lot of basements, including mine. Paul uses a similar metaphor in Romans 5:5, where he speaks of the love of God poured out in our hearts abundantly by the Holy Spirit given to us. When God the Spirit takes up residence in our hearts, He brings God's love into our lives. God's love, however, is not intended to remain within us. It is to overflow to others.

In Jonathan Edwards' work, *The End for Which God Created the World,* the great 18th century theologian uses the concept of overflowing to explain creation. He is countering the idea that God created the world because there was some lack in Him that needed to be remedied. Instead, the creation of man and all else was the overflow of God's perfections. "It is no sign of deficiency in a river that it overflows its banks."

This overflowing God enters the life of a believer at his or her salvation and intends to flow through the believer to others. Indeed, others will know that we are Christians because we love one another, as Christ teaches us in John 13:35. In the immediate context, Paul has modeled this idea for the Philippians. He longs for the Philippians with the very love of Christ. Now, he is praying that they will love each other with that very same love, that it will flow out of them to their partners in the faith.

Of course, Paul does not specify the object of the love in this prayer. They should also overflow in love to God Himself and to the lost around them. Love that is not demonstrated is like a stagnant pool. Paul wants our love to be like a rushing river.

Discerning Love
v. 9b "… in knowledge and all judgment;"

We must not fall into the trap of viewing love as merely an emotional response to those around us or as mere sentimentality. Christ's love is never just good feelings.

Paul guards against such a conception by qualifying his prayer. He wants the love of the Philippians to overflow in a very specific direction: in all knowledge and judgment or discernment. The word for judgment is a NT *hapax legomenon* but occurs regularly in the Greek translation of Proverbs, where it means "that practical understanding which is keenly aware of the circumstances of an action."[5] Paul is praying that the Philippians' love would be continually increasing in wisdom and practical insight, that is, that it would manifest itself in ever more mature and godly ways.

There is always a multitude of ways that we can show love to someone. Which is the best? In our loving, we need to know when to console, when to confront, when to rejoice with those who are rejoicing, when to mourn with those who are mourning, etc. The word *all* in this context may indicate that we need knowledge and insight in all different kinds of situations. Suppose we gave our children ice cream for dinner every night because we wanted to show love to them; this would not be insightful love.

What is the best way that you can love your roommate or coworker, friend or loved one? Does she need encouragement? Does he need confrontation of his bad attitude? God alone can give us this wisdom, and we should pray for ourselves and others that He grant it to us.

Approving the Important
10a "That ye may approve things that are excellent;"

Next, Paul expresses the purpose (or, perhaps, result) of their insightful love. The word translated "approve" means to examine something, pass

---

[5] P. T. O'Brien, *The Epistles to the Philippians,* NIGTC (Grand Rapids: Wm. B. Eerdmans, 1991), 77.

judgment on it, and give approval. For example, Romans 12:2 speaks of having our thinking renewed so that we will approve the will of God in our lives.

What are we approving here? Paul uses a very interesting word. The Stoics and Cynics were engaged in controversy at the time over matters of apparent moral indifference, which they called *adiaphora.* Is there moral significance to when you get up in the morning, what color toga you wear, whether you are a doctor or a dentist, etc.? This is a perennial discussion among Christians too. How do we determine what to do relative to matters not specifically addressed in Scripture via precept or clear principle? We often turn to Romans 14-15 or 1 Cor. 8-10 to discuss this issue of Christian liberty and how to handle matters of moral ambivalence. But I've discovered that the toughest part of the discussion is not the principles those passages teach. It's determining what issues are up for discussion.

Paul uses the word *diaphora* here. He wants the Philippians to have insightful love so that they can determine what is important and approve it. A paraphrase, the New Living Translation, gives an insightful rendering here: "For I want you to understand what really matters." This type of loving discernment will help us avoid the little controversies that can destroy our unity. "We're about to fight about _____. Before we do, let's ask a simple question: Is it really all that important?"

So far, then, Paul has prayed that the Philippians will have overflowing love that is channeled by discernment and results in figuring out what really matters in life.

Genuine and Blameless
v. 10b "that ye may be sincere and without offense till the day of Christ;"

Paul adds another purpose clause. Why does our love need to overflow in an insightful way such that we learn how to approve the things that really matter? So that we can be sincere and blameless until Christ returns.

These are two of Paul's favorite words. "Sincere" "is an interesting word that speaks of examining something in the light of the sun to discover that it is pure or genuine. It is like taking a garment out into the sunlight to examine it to determine if it is spotless."[6] You've probably heard that it described pottery that was free of wax intended to hide cracks and blemishes.

Do we live in such a way that we could bare our thoughts, motives, and deepest desires in the plain sight of God and others without embarrassment or shame? That's a tall order, but that's what Paul desires for these believers. Referring again to our athletic metaphor, when various regulating bodies announce random drug tests, it is interesting to see how some athletes angrily resist, while others cheerfully welcome the scrutiny. For believers, whether we wish it or not, God is always evaluating our innermost selves, and Paul's desire for us is that we have nothing to hide.

Paul also wants believers to be blameless, a word that refers to our testimony before others (this is the heading of the description of the godly pastor in 1 Tim. 3:2).

Both of these words hint at our standing in the fellowship of believers. As we come together in the ministry of the gospel, we are real, transparent people who live in such a way that we do not throw stumbling blocks before our brethren.

Fruit-Bearing
v. 11a "Being filled with the fruits of righteousness,"

What will sincere and blameless Christians look like? They will bear fruit, and that fruit will consist of righteousness, which means godly conduct. Notice how Paul sees love and holiness as partners. As love overflows these believers' lives in wise channels, it produces holy living.

Some have contrasted love and holiness as though these two attributes are inevitably in tension with one another. However, God is perfect love and perfectly holy, and His attributes are in perfect harmony. Therefore, to the extent that our love is God-like, it will be holy love; and to the extent that our holiness is God-like, it will be loving holiness. If our

---

[6] David Whitcomb, New Testament Baptist Church, Greer, South Carolina (2006).

holiness is harsh or arrogant, it is not genuine. If our love is indulgent or worldly, it is not the real thing.

Paul is praying for professing believers. God has declared them righteous in Christ and is producing fruit in their lives to demonstrate their righteous standing. Some of that fruit is listed in Gal. 5:22-23 (the fruit of the Spirit); 2 Peter 1:5-7 (a symphony of virtues); and James 3:17-18 (the wisdom that is from above). If we are the real deal—sincere and without offense—we will see fruit being produced in our lives.

Accomplished by Christ
v. 11b "which are by Jesus Christ,"

Paul now adds that the Philippians themselves are not the source of their fruit. Jesus Christ is producing this fruit by His Spirit in their lives. Again, the reason Paul can pray so confidently for the Philippians is because he knows God is at work in their lives producing righteousness through the finished work of Jesus Christ.

Jesus Christ is the vine—we are the branches. "It is no longer I that live, but Christ lives in me," Paul claims.[7] "For me to live is Christ" is Paul's great motto.[8]

How did Christ live? His life consisted of overflowing love that knew best how to help people because He lived for what was important, was genuine and blameless, and produced the fruit of righteousness. Paul is praying that we be Christ-like.

To the Glory of God
v. 11c "unto the glory and praise of God."

As Paul so often does, he attaches an ultimate purpose. He completes his wish-prayer with an explanation of why Jesus Christ is producing righteousness in the lives of His people. "The goal of their being filled and being blameless is not ultimately that they receive salvation, but rather

---

[7] Galatians 2:20.

[8] Philippians 1:21.

13

that God is recognized and praised for who [He] is."[9] It is fitting that God should get all the glory, because He is doing all the work. Our overflowing love, discernment, genuineness, and fruitfulness are being produced in us by the Spirit, were procured for us by Jesus Christ, and were planned for us by God the Father in His eternal, wise counsels. The Triune God deserves all the glory!

Conclusion

So, how's your joy doing? You will experience joy when you are experiencing overflowing love, discernment, and fruitfulness with the result that God is being glorified in your life. That was Paul's prayer for the Philippian believers, and it should be our prayer for one another and the main pursuit of our lives.

---

[9] Jerry L. Sumney, *Philippians: A Greek Student's Intermediate Reader* (Peabody, MA: Hendrickson, 2007), 16.

Joy in the Furtherance of the Gospel

Philippians 1:12-18 | Dr. Fred Moritz

12 But I would ye should understand, brethren, that the things which happened unto me have fallen out rather unto the furtherance of the gospel; 13 So that my bonds in Christ are manifest in all the palace, and in all other places; 14 And many of the brethren in the Lord, waxing confident by my bonds, are much more bold to speak the word without fear. 15 Some indeed preach Christ even of envy and strife; and some also of good will: 16 The one preach Christ of contention, not sincerely, supposing to add affliction to my bonds: 17 But the other of love, knowing that I am set for the defence of the gospel. 18 What then? notwithstanding, every way, whether in pretense, or in truth, Christ is preached; and I therein do rejoice, yea, and will rejoice.

Introduction

God's goal for His work in the world and His goal for believers is the same – that we should be to the praise of His glory. God *planned* and *provided* salvation in Christ "to the praise of the glory of his grace, wherein he hath made us accepted in the beloved" (Eph. 1:6). God *purposes* that believers live to bring glory to him – "That we should be to the praise of his glory, who first trusted in Christ." (Eph. 1:12). God *promises* that all who know Christ possess eternal life. The presence of the Holy Spirit in the believer's life "is the earnest of our inheritance until the redemption of the purchased possession, unto the praise of his glory" (Eph. 1:14).

In his prayer for the Philippians, Paul asked God that believers would be "filled with the fruits of righteousness unto the glory and praise of God" (Phil. 1:11). He desired that the believers in Philippi would glorify God.

Paul's primary purpose in writing this letter was to thank the Philippians for the gift they had sent him upon learning of his detention at Rome (1:5; 4:10–19). However, he makes use of this occasion to fulfill several other desires: (1) to report on his own circumstances (1:12–26; 4:10–19); (2) to encourage the Philippians to stand firm in the face of persecution and rejoice regardless of circumstances (1:27–30; 4:4); (3) to exhort them to humility and unity (2:1–11; 4:2–5); (4) to commend Timothy and Epaphroditus to the Philippian church (2:19–30); and (5) to warn the Philippians against the Judaizers (legalists) and antinomians (libertines) among them (Ch. 3).[10]

In these verses the apostle reported to the Philippians on his own circumstances. He explained his circumstances (v. 12-14). He introduced the opposition of his detractors (v. 15-17).

Paul affirmed that God has used the difficult circumstances of his arrest and imprisonment to further the cause of the gospel, and he rejoices in that fact. *We must understand what it means to work for the furtherance (or progress) of the gospel.*

Persecution for the Furtherance of the Gospel
v. 12 the things which happened unto me

These events began with the ministry in Philippi that Luke described in Acts 16:9-40. A group of women, both natural Jews and proselytes, gathered at the riverside on a Sabbath (Saturday) morning to worship God. Paul, Luke, and the others in his group gathered with them. Paul spoke, and Scripture records the tender account of God opening Lydia's heart. She and those of her household received the message of Christ and were baptized (v. 15). Also, a slave girl who was a demon-possessed fortune teller was delivered from her bondage. Those who profited from her divination stirred up the populace. Paul and Silas were arrested, beaten, and jailed.

God gave grace to the beaten preachers, and they sang and prayed at midnight (v. 25-30). God sent an earthquake. The jailer thought the prisoners had escaped at the cost of his life, and he was stunned to find them there. The Philippian jailer and his household were saved and baptized that very night. From these experiences people were saved and the church at Philippi was begun.

---

[10] https://www.biblica.com/resources/scholar-notes/niv-study-bible/intro-to-philippians/ Accessed September 23, 2018.

Scripture records: "And they went out of the prison and entered into *the house of* Lydia: and when they had seen the brethren, they comforted them, and departed" (Acts 16:40). Paul spoke to the Philippian believers with authority when he said: "the things *which happened* unto me have fallen out rather unto the furtherance of the gospel." God used suffering and persecution to further the gospel testimony in Philippi.

Paul's affirmation also includes his ministry after Philippi. That ministry would take him to Athens, Corinth, Ephesus, and Jerusalem. He then appealed to Caesar and was taken to Rome. He was preparing for his trial when he wrote from the Roman prison saying: "the things *which happened* unto me have fallen out rather unto the furtherance of the gospel" (v. 12).

These events resulted in the furtherance of the gospel (v. 13). His bonds were "in Christ" – he was specifically incarcerated and on trial for his testimony and ministry as a Christian. The Praetorian (palace guards) knew his imprisonment and trial was because of his service for Christ. It is possible that he was chained to a guard while in prison. Paul knew that because of his situation the testimony of Christ went beyond the praetorian to "all other places." He lived for Christ and testified of him, even in this situation.

Boldness in the Furtherance of the Gospel
v. 14 And many of the brethren in the Lord, waxing confident by my bonds, are much more bold to speak the word without fear.

Paul informs us that his imprisonment emboldened many believers to speak boldly of Christ: "And many of the brethren in the Lord, waxing confident by my bonds, are much more bold to speak the word without fear" (v. 14).

We think persecution would intimidate believers, keeping them from speaking for Christ. But this ordeal had just the opposite effect on "many brothers." It had a profound [widespread?] impact on them, and they "waxed confident," or were "persuaded" by his confinement. His suffering prompted Christians in Rome to "speak the word without fear."

We do not think of boldness in the face of persecution. Our instinct would be to protect ourselves when faced with danger or, in this case, with

17

persecution. This trial had just the opposite effect. This godly boldness seems to have characterized New Testament Christians when facing persecution. Acts 3:1-10 relates the story of Peter and John healing a man who was lame from birth. Peter preached the message of Christ's death, resurrection, and power to save (Acts 3:12-26). The two apostles were detained, and the next day "the priests, and the captain of the temple, and the Sadducees" questioned them about the miracle (Acts 4:1-7). Peter and John declared the man was healed "by the name of Jesus Christ" (Acts 4:8-12). The authorities noted the boldness that characterized the two men. They also understood the Apostles were neither educated men nor specialists in the law. They concluded their boldness resulted because they had been with Jesus (Acts 4:13). They threatened the two and commanded them to speak no more in Christ's name (v. 17, 18, 21).

Facing the threat of suffering, the early church prayed. Christians did not ask God to protect them from persecution. Rather, they prayed: "And now, Lord, behold their threatenings: and grant unto thy servants, that with all boldness they may speak thy word" (v. 29).
God heard and answered their prayer! "And when they had prayed, the place was shaken where they were assembled together; and they were all filled with the Holy Ghost, and they spake the word of God with boldness" (v. 31). They prayed for boldness, and God gave them boldness.

We must learn spiritual lessons from these accounts.

1) First, we can pray for boldness to speak God's Word. The Apostle Paul asked the Ephesian believers to pray for him. He was a prisoner in Rome when he wrote to them, yet he did not pray, nor ask them to pray, for his persecution to be alleviated. Rather, he asked them to pray for God to embolden him to make the gospel known: "And for me, that utterance may be given unto me, that I may open my mouth boldly, to make known the mystery of the gospel, For which I am an ambassador in bonds: that therein I may speak boldly, as I ought to speak" (Eph. 6:19-20).

2) Second, we should take courage that God will give us boldness to give the gospel even when we face opposition for our faith. Paul prayed for boldness to make Christ known from a Roman prison.

His faith eventually cost his life, but he prayed for boldness to preach Christ in any circumstance.

Detractors and the Furtherance of the Gospel
v. 17 of envy and strife

Some in Paul's day preached Christ "of envy and strife" (v 15). "Envy (φθόνον [*phthonon*]) is an old word and an old sin, and strife (ἔρις [*eris*]) is more rivalry than schism. *It is petty and personal jealousy* of Paul's power and prowess by the Judaizers in Rome"[11] [Emphasis mine.]

Others knew the apostle was set for the defense of the gospel. *Defense* is a legal technical term, a speech in defense of oneself, a *reply, a verbal defense* (2Tim. 4.16); *defense* is also used as a religious technical term *defense* of the gospel message from false teaching (PH 1.7)"[12]

It is almost inevitable that we will face some form of opposition in the cause of Christ. Don't bring such opposition on yourself by foolish words or actions. Determine to be faithful to the Lord when the opposition arises.

Joy at the Furtherance of the Gospel
v. 18 What then? notwithstanding, every way, whether in pretence, or in truth, Christ is preached; and I therein do rejoice, yea, and will rejoice.

Paul could say that even if these detractors were active, and despite their motives, they were still preaching Christ. He knew he served the Lord in truth. Thus, he could rejoice that Christ was preached. He preached the message of Christ as he received it. Believers in Rome came to Christ and thus lived for Christ and testified of Him. His detractors, moved by personal jealousy, still preached the message of the cross of Christ. Through it all, the apostle *rejoiced* that Christ was preached.

---

[11] A.T. Robertson, *Word Pictures in the New Testament* (Nashville, TN: Broadman Press, 1933), Philippians 1:15.

[12] Ibid.

Conclusion

We must devote ourselves to working for the furtherance (or progress) of the gospel. Be a witness and soul-winner now. Give your life to serve the Lord wherever he puts you. Be faithful to Him in every circumstance, even if it means persecution. Rejoice in giving the gospel to others.

Live Worthy of Your Gospel Identity

Philippians 1:19-30 | Dr. Bryan Brock

19 For I know that this shall turn to my salvation through your prayer, and the supply of the Spirit of Jesus Christ, 20 According to my earnest expectation and my hope, that in nothing I shall be ashamed, but that with all boldness, as always, so now also Christ shall be magnified in my body, whether it be by life, or by death. 21 For to me to live is Christ, and to die is gain. 22 But if I live in the flesh, this is the fruit of my labour: yet what I shall choose I wot not. 23 For I am in a strait betwixt two, having a desire to depart, and to be with Christ; which is far better: 24 Nevertheless to abide in the flesh is more needful for you 25 And having this confidence, I know that I shall abide and continue with you all for your furtherance and joy of faith; 26 That your rejoicing may be more abundant in Jesus Christ for me by my coming to you again. 27 Only let your conversation be as it becometh the gospel of Christ: that whether I come and see you, or else be absent, I may hear of your affairs, that ye stand fast in one spirit, with one mind striving together for the faith of the gospel; 28 And in nothing terrified by your adversaries: which is to them an evident token of perdition, but to you of salvation, and that of God. 29 For unto you it is given in the behalf of Christ, not only to believe on him, but also to suffer for his sake; 30 Having the same conflict which ye saw in me, and now hear to be in me.

Paul leverages his close personal relationship with the Philippian believers to encourage and exhort them. This is more than just human relationship, however; Christ is involved too (He's referenced nine times in these verses). And as an added layer, Paul writes to them in a context where the Christian community stands isolated in the sweeping current of a unified and hostile culture!

That is why at the rhetorical and theological heart of this section (and possibly the entire letter), Paul appeals to their identity in the gospel— "Only let your conversation be as it becometh the gospel of Christ" (v. 27). The word "conversation" is different than the normal word for conduct. This is a word that literally means, "live out your *citizenship*." It's the same word that's used in 3:20, "our citizenship is in heaven"!

This is a direct answer to the current day culture that elevated Roman citizenship as the ultimate identity. Roman morality said that 'as long as

Caesar is your god' you are moral (your depravity under the lordship of Caesar is moral). Roman superiority said that as long as you are Roman you are to be valued. Roman identity entitled you to freedom, rights, and respect.

But before we judge Roman culture too harshly, doesn't our culture do the same thing? Our culture dangles certain identities before us—if you want to be accepted, if you want to measure up to true morality, if you want to be valued—identify with us! In this entire section, Paul gives one command, "Live out your citizenship" (v. 27); and listen carefully to its adverb— "only" and its compliment— "worthy of the gospel of Christ."

Brothers and sisters, can I encourage and exhort you with the same needed call—in the midst of a crooked and perverse generation will you strive by the grace of God to make it your mission to Live Worthy of your Gospel Identity"?

Gospel Worthy Perspective of Deliverance
vv. 19-20 For I know that this shall turn to my salvation (i.e. deliverance...)

When Paul says, "I know that this shall turn to my deliverance," it would be natural to assume that he means "deliverance from prison & death." Right now he is imprisoned in Rome, and the end of verses 20–21 make it clear he's at a place where death is a real possibility! It is so easy to want and prioritize *that* kind of deliverance! But what Paul truly means by "deliverance" is revealed in verse 20, "That in nothing I shall be ashamed." Christian, this testimony reveals what it means to "live worthy of the gospel!"

Our ultimate deliverance is not escaping our circumstances, but rather in remaining faithful to Christ regardless of how difficult our situation! Paul reveals his overarching goal in verse 20b that no matter the personal outcome, Christ will be magnified![13] And in the lead up to this goal he testifies that this is what we should pray for and be praying for each

---

[13] v. 20b ...that in nothing I shall be ashamed, but *that* with all boldness, as always, *so* now also Christ shall be magnified in my body, whether *it be* by life, or by death.

other about (v. 19a),[14] this is what the Spirit is working in us for,[15] and this should be our highest priority (v. 20a)![16]

In your life-challenges, crisis, or loss, what's your priority? "God, fix this. Free me. Deliver me." Or, "Lord, help me to be faithful. Be magnified by life or by death. God, please give me aid… but as you give, may I always treasure You, the Giver above all!" *Gospel worthy identity has that perspective of deliverance, but we also need…*

Gospel Worthy Passion for Christ
vv. 21-26

All our life should be about Christ. This is what Paul intends when he pens these famous words, "For to me to live is Christ, and to die is gain" (v. 21). "To live is Christ" must be more than just a cliché; it's more than just a tack-on to our other 'priorities' of life! *What about gain?* It's the fruit of grace-enabled labor until I see the smile of my Savior (vv. 22–23).[17] That is, it is a similar concept to the cycle of farming and harvest. Living for Christ is the labor in the fields, and gain is the harvest. So, by Paul's personal testimony the believer is encouraged that in life we labor for Christ, and in death the harvest is the gain of Christ. Both are the allotment of our Master, and after a life of service, both are desirable for the Christian.

There is an added dimension to the believer's willingness (or even eagerness) to enter his reward, and that is the point that Paul makes in verses 24–26 – that other people are part of the equation. Although

---

[14] v. 19a For I know that this shall turn to my salvation through your prayer…

[15] v. 19b For I know that this shall turn to my salvation through your prayer, and the supply of the Spirit of Jesus Christ, (cf. Rom. 8:26-27 "…the Spirit intercedes for the saints according to the will of God")

[16] v. 20a According to my earnest expectation and *my* hope,

[17] vv. 22-23 But if I live in the flesh, this *is* the fruit of my labour: yet what I shall choose I wot not. [23] For I am in a strait betwixt two, having a desire to depart, and to be with Christ; which is far better:

others need us, the perspective of the Christian laborer is that "to live for Christ" is to help people grow in Christ and find their joy in Christ![18]

Who are you investing in to grow their faith ('until Christ be formed in' them—Gal. 4:19), to help their joy to be in Christ? Don't wimp out. It may be uncomfortable, but it's for Jesus! This is what it means to say, "For me, to live is Christ and to die is gain." *This is a gospel worthy passion for Christ, but we also see that we need...*

Gospel Worthy Partnership for the Gospel
v. 27 Only live as citizens worthy of the gospel of Christ: that whether I come and see you, or else be absent, I may hear of your affairs, that ye stand fast in one spirit, with one mind striving together for the faith of the gospel;

Each one who has been saved by the gospel needs to live worthy of the gospel—this reminds us of the real ethical requirements of the gospel. Every believer has a gospel mandate for how we live! "Only live as citizens worthy of the gospel of Christ" (v. 27). This isn't just external; it's all the time—"That whether I come and see you, or else be absent, I may hear of your affairs" (v. 27b). This also isn't simply done as isolated individuals. The gospel creates partnership—unity in the gospel (v. 27c)![19] True unity ("in one spirit") *only* happens when we've believed the *same* gospel (Paul warns about "another gospel" in Gal. 1)!

And of course, gospel worthy partnerships are *for* the gospel (v. 27d).[20] We partner for the purity of the gospel "with one mind" or in full agreement. Every church, and any Christian organization with a gospel mission cannot forget to demand an allegiance to the "faith which was once delivered unto the saints" (Jude 3). But what we're seeing more and more are organizations that profess to be "for the gospel" that are

---

[18] vv. 24-26 Nevertheless to abide in the flesh *is* more needful for you. 25 And having this confidence, I know that I shall abide and continue with you all for your furtherance and joy of faith; 26 That your rejoicing may be more abundant in Jesus Christ for me by my coming to you again.

[19] v. 27c ...that ye stand fast in one spirit,

[20] v. 27d ...with one mind striving together (side-by-side) for the faith of the gospel;

emphasizing what the gospel does, and de-emphasizing what the Gospel is! By the way, this is why local churches should never outsource their responsibility to be the "pillar and ground of the truth" (1 Tim 3:15). That is why MBU emphasizes the support of local churches in our mission!

The gospel must be the main thing. We must know it, believe it, guard it, and proclaim it! This is God's purpose for putting us in partnership with other believers; this is the mandate to the worldwide body of true believers, but more specifically this is the calling for all of us in our local NT church partnerships. And as we will see, this kind of true partnership for the gospel will put us at cross purposes to the world.

Gospel Worthy Peace in the Face of Opposition
vv. 28-30

Evangelism was a dangerous thing in a Roman-centric culture. *Why?* Because it undermined the god of Rome—Caesar. Evangelism is just as dangerous today because we are directly undercutting the gods of this age—self-esteem, pluralism, society-approved-perversion, mob-decided-morality, and any identity that exalts itself against the knowledge of God (2 Cor. 10:5)!

We can be encouraged, however, because opposition for Christ is eternally better than the alternative. In verse 28a Paul encourages, "And in nothing terrified by your adversaries." This begs the question, what will keep us from being terrified? The implied answer it *the gospel*. And as believers experience peace in the storm of opposition, this will be "to them an evident token of perdition, but to you of salvation, and that of God" (v. 28b). Peace in opposition points to the truth of the gospel we proclaim which speaks peace to believers and condemnation to rejecters.

We also see that opposition for Christ comes with all the goodness of God behind it! In verse 29 Paul encourages, "For unto you it is given (*charis* – grace) in the behalf of Christ, not only to believe on him, but also to suffer for his sake." Have you ever heard anyone complain/brag? Imagine a teenage basketball fan complaining, "Whew, this weekend was rough; I got some painful blisters. Yeah, I was playing some hoops with LeBron James at the YMCA and it was pretty rough on my feet." The downside of that story is nothing compared to the overall experience of playing basketball with one of the most famous players of all time!

25

So, when we say, "I've suffered a bit for His sake... because He's *my* Savior by faith," there's no doubt that truly—it's all good! We can't say that faith is grace (God's underserved goodness—of which He is the author and finisher), and not also recognize that opposition is our lot by the all-good hand of our sovereign Father!

This also puts us in good company. Paul says in verse 30, "Having the same conflict which ye saw in me, and now hear to be in me." And of course, we are reminded of Jesus' encouragement, "Blessed are ye, when men shall revile you, and persecute you, and shall say all manner of evil against you falsely, for my sake. *Rejoice, and be exceeding glad*: for great is your reward in heaven: for so persecuted they the prophets which were before you" (Matt. 5:11-12).

Conclusion

Our identity is not of this earth. "Our citizenship is in heaven"! Therefore, "Only live as citizens worthy of the gospel of Christ." Gospel identity is not just a position but a personal, progressive calling which encompasses the following: gospel worthy perspective of deliverance; gospel worthy passion for Christ; gospel worthy partnership for the gospel; and gospel worthy peace in the face of opposition! *Will you live worthy of your gospel identity?*

The Worthy Walk

Philippians 2:1-11 | Dr. David Saxon

¹If there be therefore any consolation in Christ, if any comfort of love, if any fellowship of the Spirit, if any bowels and mercies, ² Fulfil ye my joy, that ye be likeminded, having the same love, being of one accord, of one mind. ³ Let nothing be done through strife or vainglory; but in lowliness of mind let each esteem other better than themselves. ⁴ Look not every man on his own things, but every man also on the things of others. ⁵ Let this mind be in you, which was also in Christ Jesus: ⁶ Who, being in the form of God, thought it not robbery to be equal with God: ⁷ But made himself of no reputation, and took upon him the form of a servant, and was made in the likeness of men: ⁸ And being found in fashion as a man, he humbled himself, and became obedient unto death, even the death of the cross. ⁹ Wherefore God also hath highly exalted him, and given him a name which is above every name: ¹⁰ That at the name of Jesus every knee should bow, of things in heaven, and things in earth, and things under the earth; ¹¹ And that every tongue should confess that Jesus Christ is Lord, to the glory of God the Father.

In Philippians 1:19-30, we saw that Paul lived his life centered on Christ. For Paul, to live was Christ and to die was more Christ. It didn't matter, then, whether he lived or died, as long as Christ was magnified in his life.

In verse 27 Paul then urged the Philippians to think the same way. He instructed them to let their conduct as citizens of heaven be worthy of the gospel of Christ. As noted earlier in our series, the idea of worthiness is fitness to a standard. The standard was the gospel of Christ, and they were to live in such a way that their lives aligned with the gospel. This probably implies two things: the gospel is enabling their lives and their lives are reflecting the gospel.

This is often how a standard works. If I am seeking a straight line, then I use a ruler—the standard. When I draw worthy of the standard, i.e., straight, two things are true: the ruler has clearly enabled my straight drawing, and, second, anyone wanting to know what straight looks like can tell, not only by looking at the ruler but also by looking at my line.

All of this sounds like really good theory. My life is Christ; my citizenship is in heaven; my walk is in alignment with the gospel. Practically speaking, what does such living actually look like?

Paul will devote the entirety of chapter 2 to answering that question. Verses 1-4 give a powerful summary of the worthy walk, and then Paul provides four illustrations of the worthy walk. Verses 5-11 display the ultimate example: Jesus Christ. Verses 12-18 speak of Paul himself, who, like Christ, has poured himself out for the Philippians. In verses 19-24, Paul speaks of Timothy, who is likeminded with Paul. And the last six verses of the chapter (25-30) use a Philippian brother, Epaphroditus, to illustrate this theology.

Philippians 2:1-11 I believe, answers three questions about the gospel-aligned walk: why, what, and how. Why should I walk this way (v. 1)? What does it mean to walk this way (vv. 2-4)? And how do I walk this way (vv. 5-11)?

This is an extremely familiar text. When I attended a Christian college, I believe the two texts I heard preached most often were Romans 12:1-2 and this text. As I was discussing this text with my youngest son, who is now in seminary, I told him that I was preaching on one of the two texts I had heard most in college. He immediately guessed Romans 12 and Philippians 2. Therefore, with your indulgence (and with apologies to Paul), I'm going to take the text in reverse order: how, what, why.

How to Live the Gospel
vv. 5-11

Verse 5 begins with a command: have the same mind that Christ had. The word *mind* refers to attitude or perspective. "Have the same approach to life that Christ had." How did Christ approach life?

In one of the works of Andrew Murray, he collected the following samples of Christ's attitude from the Gospel of John:

- John 5:30 – *I can of mine own self do nothing: … I seek not mine own will, but the will of the Father which hath sent me.*
- John 5:41 – *I receive no honor from men* (or, literally, "I do not accept praise from men.")
- John 6:38 – *For I came down from heaven, not to do mine own will, but the will of him that sent me.*

- John 7:16 – *My doctrine is not mine, but his that sent me.*
- John 7:28 – *I have not come of myself.*
- John 8:28 – *I do nothing of myself, but as my Father hath taught me, I speak these things.*
- John 8:42 – *Neither came I of myself, but he sent me.*
- John 8:50 – *I seek not mine own glory.*
- John 14:10 – *The words that I speak unto you, I speak not of myself: but the Father that dwelleth in me, he doeth the works.*
- John 14:24 – *The word which you hear is not mine, but the Father's which sent me.*

Murray goes on to say,

> [Christ] was nothing that God might be all. He resigned himself to the Father's will and power that He might work through Him. Of His own power, His own will, His own glory, His whole mission with its works and teaching—of all this, He said, I am nothing. I have given myself to the Father to work; He is all.[21]

So Christ is the model for our obeying this mandate. What was this attitude that Christ modeled for us? Paul explores this concept in verses 6-8 in a magnificent poem.

Our purpose in this chapter is not to explore this poem in depth (O'Brien's commentary on Philippians devotes 85 pages to it).[22] But note quickly who it is that is submitting Himself entirely to the will of His Father.

1) First, He already existed in the form of God, which means He had a prior existence with the very nature of God.

2) Second, He "thought it not robbery to be equal with God" means that He did not grasp equality with God and use it for His own advantage. The idea is not that He tried to steal equality from God, but rather that He had equality with God and had every right

---

[21] Andrew Murray, *Humility: The Journey Toward Holiness* (Minneapolis: Bethany House, 2001), 32.

[22] P. T. O'Brien, *The Epistles to the Philippians,* NIGTC (Grand Rapids: Wm. B. Eerdmans, 1991), 186-271.

to use it to prevent discomfort, suffering, etc. but He willingly chose to give up those rights.

3) Third, He "emptied himself" *(made himself of no reputation)*. Such an expression immediately raises a difficult question: of what did He empty Himself? Paul answers that question in the text: He emptied Himself "by taking upon himself the form of a slave." His emptying did not involve giving up any aspect of his Godhead but rather taking on something, namely, servanthood. You and I becoming servants would involve no emptying, but it is breathtaking that one who had the essence of God and equality with God enrobed Himself with frail humanity.

4) Finally, He "took the form of a slave and was made in the likeness of men." As O'Brien well says, "He did not exchange the nature or form of God for that of a slave; instead, he displayed the nature or form of God in the nature or form of a slave."[23]

When my wife and I moved from South Carolina to Watertown in 1999 to work at Maranatha Baptist University, we contacted the school to see if a few young men could help us move in. We had four small children and my wife's parents along, and we were moving into a three-story duplex about half an hour from campus. What we did not realize is that MBU's (Maranatha Baptist Bible College at the time) campus is a ghost town during the summers, with very few students staying to work. On the day of our move, a car pulled up with helpers. To our shock and chagrin, out stepped the president of the college, the head of the Bible Department, another senior administrator, and a young man who worked in the garage. At least, there was one young man! When we tried to get them to just transfer our furniture into the garage, they insisted that they move everything exactly where it was needed. The president's wife later brought us dinner for our first day. We were not slow to learn the moral of this story (although, they weren't trying to teach us a moral; they were simply serving): these administrators did not cease being senior administrators, but they were willing to add menial service to their résumés. In so doing, they showed me—a lowly faculty member—what service at MBU was to look like.

---

[23] Ibid., 223-224.

Christ's humbling led all the way to the cross. This is the ultimate example of service: the greatest possible Being making the greatest possible sacrifice on behalf of the least worthy and least able to reciprocate. At verse 9 the poem surprisingly breaks away from describing service to picturing exaltation. In some ways, this relates uniquely to Christ, but I believe Paul also intends application to his readers.

First consider the poem's application to Christ. "Wherefore" indicates that Christ's exaltation was directly connected to His humiliation. Notice that the Actor is now the Father, for the first time in the poem. Christ submitted humbly to God's purposes, but now God is undertaking for Christ and exalting Him. The verb "highly exalted" means "to raise to the highest position," and is in a tense that probably implies that this result has already been accomplished. Christ rose from the dead, ascended into Heaven, and sits at the right hand of God. He is sovereign over all, and one day He will return and exert His sovereignty on this earth. Paul alludes to Isaiah 45:22-23. If the humiliation of Christ has caused anyone to doubt whether or not He is God, the final scene will remove all doubt. While Christ graciously showed us God's love and compassion through the Incarnation and the Atonement, one day He will demonstrate God's sovereign omnipotence by forcing to their knees His enemies and ours.

Therefore, verses 9-11 express the reward of His service. We believers will share in this reward as well, and I believe Paul wants us to see that implication. Later in Philippians is a text, 3:20-21, that has numerous verbal similarities to 2:9-11. In this text we are promised that one day, our bodies of humiliation will be replaced with glorious bodies like Christ's. The verses in our text are intended to encourage us as we are called upon to humble ourselves, that one day we too will be exalted.

Is it appropriate for us to look forward to our own exaltation? It must be, since the Scriptures repeatedly hold out this future prospect as our blessed hope. The promise of heaven and future reward is given believers in scores of passages in both testaments.

This is not a mercenary hope, however, for two reasons. C. S. Lewis explains in his essay "The Weight of Glory"[24] that prizes may or may not be mercenary. A general who fights for victory is not mercenary; the general who fights so that he can run for political office is. The husband who marries for love is not mercenary; the husband who marries for money is. When the prize is the natural consummation of the activity so that it is essentially part of the activity, then it is not mercenary. And that's what our rewards in heaven will be. After humbly pursuing God all our lives, the reward will be we get Him.

The other reason this hope is not mercenary and will not make us proud is that we will see with stark clarity that it is not deserved. Unlike Christ, whose exaltation was the restoration of the glory He had throughout eternity, our exaltation will itself be a manifestation of the incredible grace of God. As Richard Baxter expressed it centuries ago, "Doubtless it will be our everlasting admiration that so rich a crown should fit the head of so vile a sinner."[25] After all, what this passage is teaching is that my exaltation will eventually mean I am on my knees worshiping King Jesus. As a former pastor of mine used to say, "Humility will overtake everyone."[26]

The truly humble recognize that only Jesus deserves worship. If even He, who deserves exaltation, emptied Himself and took on servanthood, who are we to make ourselves the center of our private universes and demand that others serve us? Jesus has shown us once and for all how to live the gospel!

What Living the Gospel Looks Like
vv. 2-4

Earlier in verse 2, Paul commanded the Philippians to "fulfill his joy," or "make his joy complete." In a section that is focused on humility and the

---

[24] C. S. Lewis, "The Weight of Glory" in *The Weight of Glory and Other Addresses* (New York: HarperCollins Publishers, 1980 reprint of 1949 original), 25-46.

[25] Richard Baxter, *The Saints' Everlasting Rest* (Welwyn, Herts., England: Evangelical Press, 1978), 59.

[26] David Whitcomb, New Testament Baptist Church, Greer, South Carolina.

corporate unity of the church, why would Paul make the command relate to his own joy? Wouldn't it be incongruous if I told my kids that I wanted them to think about others all the time, so that *I* would be happier? Perhaps, Paul is teaching the Philippians that they will find joy only as they seek the joy of others. Paul's heart is wrapped around the Philippians; if they love Paul, they will want to obey these commands so that he will be happy with them. If I said to my children, "Make me happy by doing your very best this semester," I wouldn't be focusing on myself and my happiness. My desire would be that they do their very best. If, however, they love me and desire my happiness, this will be a strong motive for them to work hard. So even this expression of Paul is showing us how to live for others.

Paul urges four expressions of unity that all focus on those around us: that we be likeminded, like-loved, like-souled ("of one accord"), and like-purposed ("of one mind"). We do not all think alike; we don't all love the same things; we certainly don't have identical personalities; and we don't have the same purposes and goals. How can we possibly obey these commands?

The beauty of unity in the church is that it is not uniformity—everyone playing the same musical note or playing the same position on the field or court; it is harmony. Sports fans have seen eleven men functioning as one on a soccer or football field. I recently attended a recital on MBU's campus in which four string musicians played in magnificent sync, producing beauty no one of them could have achieved. But they were obviously not all playing the same notes. The unity was achieved not only despite diversity but *by means of* diversity. That's why the Puritan theologian Jeremiah Burroughs could say, "Variety of opinion and unity of opinion are not incompatible."

Such unity, though, does involve denying self. There are no normal verbs in the Greek text of verses 3 and 4. These verses simply attach participial clauses that modify the sentence we have just studied in verses 1b and 2. There is, therefore, a very close connection between these verses.

In verses 3a and 4a, Paul lists three enemies of unity. "Strife," is selfish ambition. This word does not describe the conflict that comes from selfish ambition, but the selfish ambition itself. Nothing is more destructive of unity than turf wars, power trips, and massive egos. Second, he mentions "vainglory," which is selfish conceit. A conceited person thinks he has the right to rule others and to enforce his will on them. Finally, he speaks of "looking on one's own things," which is selfish absorption.

This third item connects with me because I have the ability to zone out everyone and everything. In the late 1990s, my wife and I and our four children lived in a very small home. Every Tuesday I would sit in the computer room, working on my dissertation. A few feet away my wife was homeschooling our five-year-old while his three-year-old brother would crawl on my lap and do other toddler-y things. I learned to block it all out. This can be a useful skill—especially, if you have a doctoral dissertation to write—but it can also be pretty dangerous. Paul warns that we all tend to focus so much on our own concerns that we ignore the needs that are all around us.

In verses 3b and 4b, Paul discusses two defenders of unity: a meek mindset – regarding others as better than oneself. This is not self-loathing but rather self-forgetfulness. I regard others as more deserving of responsibility, as more needful of blessing, as more worthy. I wish to see them growing, achieving, and excelling rather than myself. And, second, a ministry mindset – looking on the things of others. This is the perfect complement to a meek mindset. If we have real interest in the lives of others and regard them as worthy of our time and energy, we will discover needy people.

Paul is advocating a very humble, self-abnegating manner of life. Why would anyone want to live this way? It is so unnatural.

Why I Should Live the Gospel
v. 1

Paul launches this passage with a fourfold "if" – you should live this way if certain things are true of you. The nature of these expressions is that Paul believes they are true of the Philippian believers, but rather than simply affirming them, he uses a construction that invites the readers to evaluate themselves. Are these things true of me? If they are, the rest of the passage—the commands to live humble lives that emulate the Ultimate Model of humility, Jesus Christ—should be true of me as well.

All four of Paul's expressions focus on the gospel and what it has done for me.

1) First, the gospel has provided consolation in Christ. *Consolation* is a form of the word translated "Comforter" in John 14-15, describing the Spirit. In the NT, it can refer to encouragement, exhortation, comfort, or, more generally, to the help one needs in whatever distress one is facing. Notice that Paul does not say, however, that we have "consolation from Christ." We do, but that is not the point here. We have consolation because we are "in Christ." Clearly, this applies to every saved person. Because of our relationship with Christ, because we are united to Him by faith, we have the continual encouragement that arises from such a union.

2) Second, the gospel has provided comfort from love. Being united to Christ means we are loved by Christ. Nothing is more comforting than knowing Christ loves us!

3) Paul's third entailment of the gospel for believers is communion with the Spirit. *Communion* is the great word *koinonia*. Paul, in this letter, has already emphasized his fellowship with the Philippians and their fellowship with one another (1:3-8). But here what is binding them all together is that the Spirit is the Source and Sustainer of their fellowship.

4) Finally, the gospel has produced compassion and mercies. *Bowels and mercies* are synonyms that refer to compassion, tenderness, and kind affection. Most likely, Paul is repeating that we have been made the recipients of God's (or Christ's) tender compassion. This may seem repetitive, but Paul is stacking up terms to express what God has done for us.

Taken as a whole, these phrases express that "the character of Christ is imprinted" all over the assembly.[27] Have you received the consolation, comfort, communion, and compassion that come from the gospel? We

---

[27] Quoting a sermon by David Whitcomb, delivered at New Testament Baptist Church, Greer, South Carolina.

earned none of these things. They are gifts of grace. If we have—if we are saved!—then we should live in alignment with these truths. Christ has blazed the path for us—gospel living is others living—and He has given us all we need to follow that path.

Conclusion

In summary, why should I live the gospel? Because the gospel has provided magnificent benefits, none of which I earned. What does it look like to live the gospel? It looks like humbly serving others rather than living for myself. How does one live the gospel? By imitating Jesus Christ, who not only achieved the gospel by His saving acts but displayed the gospel in His attitudes of humility and self-sacrifice. The result of living the gospel will be rewards, rewards we should pursue with all our might. Nevertheless, as we find ourselves gladly prostrated before our Redeemer, the Lord Jesus Christ, we will cast our crowns at His feet, finally seeing with utmost clarity that He enabled all of our service and He alone is worthy. We will be overtaken by humility. Why not live humbly now?

Why Don't You Grow Up?

Philippians 2:12-18 | Dr. Steve Love

12 Wherefore, my beloved, as ye have always obeyed, not as in my presence only, but now much more in my absence, work out your own salvation with fear and trembling. 13 For it is God which worketh in you both to will and to do of his good pleasure. 14 Do all things without murmurings and disputings: 15 That ye may be blameless and harmless, the sons of God, without rebuke, in the midst of a crooked and perverse nation, among whom ye shine as lights in the world; 16 Holding forth the word of life; that I may rejoice in the day of Christ, that I have not run in vain, neither laboured in vain. 17 Yea, and if I be offered upon the sacrifice and service of your faith, I joy, and rejoice with you all. 18 For the same cause also do ye joy, and rejoice with me.

Our focus in the book of Philippians is the mining of truths concerning *the gospel and its implications to joy.*

- Is there anything about verse 12 that grips your conscience?
- Does the fact that God inserts the words *with fear and trembling* have any implication that this passage is to be taken seriously?
- Are the biblical graces of *fear* and *trembling* part of your spiritual toolbox and practice as a believer?

The passage in focus is the application part of what has not only been said in this chapter, but what has been said up to this point. It involves sanctification. It brings to a head this matter of what I am to do with the power of the gospel, and within the context of this book of Philippians, what part does the gospel have to do with joy in the life of a believer?

Would you consider yourself to be a growing Christian who experiences joy? If you are, what part of spiritual growth is your responsibility? What have you intentionally and meaningfully done towards your spiritual growth today? Why don't you grow up? Or why you don't grow up! This is the tension on this subject of sanctification—spiritual growth. Is it to be done by our efforts? Then where is grace? Is it to be done by grace? Then where is our effort? Do our efforts undermine the power of the gospel? Is sanctification to be seen as an either-or proposition? Our passage provides answers to these questions.

Throughout the introduction, I've intentionally asked questions as a means of making sure that we understand that we are to personally interact and experience what is being proposed within this paragraph. The truths and blessings presented in the book of Philippians are directly related to how one responds to "...working out one's salvation..." and doing so by the reliance of God's inner workings.

What are we to do?
v. 12 work out your own salvation with fear and trembling.

Now, here's the sticky part: working out your salvation is linked to obedience. Some might say that we are millennials, and we don't really like the word *obedience*, because it smacks of legalism. Listen, the WWII generation also did not like the word *obedience*. The Israelites wandering in the wilderness also did not like the word *obedience*. Adam and Eve also did not like the word *obedience,* but look at it this way: blood-bought Old Testament and New Testament believers are the only humans in all of planet earth that actually have an option to biblically obey the God of the universe, and rather than run from it, we are enabled to run toward it. Biblical obedience is a wonderfully positive concept when considering that we all descended from a long line of sinners. Our human makeup is that of being a constant sinner. Our sin nature obligates sinning, but our new nature offers the wonderful option of obedience.

We have this option because of the following reasons:
1) The power of the gospel (2:8), revealed as a progressive on-going power (1:6);
2) The glory of God (2:11), revealed who and what God is and has done (2:10);
3) The awareness of not wanting to disappoint the one who has mentored them (Paul) and not hurt the One who saved them (Jesus).

The word *beloved* is used to establish a reason for obedience —this *work out your own salvation* is not being promoted through guilt or ill motive, but through a relationship that is tight enough to be referred to as *beloved.* Because of this wonderful relationship with Paul and with God, the believers were to be working because of a wanting to please.

That ye may approve things that are excellent; that ye may be sincere and without offence till the day of Christ (1:10).

> Illustration: During my time at Maranatha I played soccer. Due to the distance, my father was only able to come and watch me play once a year. As a son, I wrestled with wanting to do well – not necessarily to show off but to do well. My motivation was not sponsored by a fear relationship with my father but a respectful relationship in which I desired to please and honor him. I was not obligated to do well because of a rule, which he imposed on me, but I had an internal obligation of wanting to please him. It was a want rather than a rule.

When our want [desire?] is gone, all the working out can only be fear-sponsored, dread-instigated and not reflective of a relationship which sponsors a working out. This obedience issue is not connected to the wrath of God but the heart of God because we are addressed as *beloved*.

4) This fear and trembling sees the weakness of self and the power of salvation (2:2b) and seeks to obey with the highest of motives (1:27). It needs to be asked because it is being presented, do we have this *fear and trembling* at the core of why and how we work out our salvation? We are to have a holy fear of our own spiritual weakness to temptation. The issue is not so much a fear of the sin, but a fear of weaknesses toward sin and disappointing God. The other is to have a trembling awareness of the power of temptation. On account of such, [you] *work out your own salvation*—that personal gift of grace given to you by the God who desires to *work in you*.

Work out carries with it the ideas of assembling the pieces, putting together, carrying it into effect. It is a mathematical, agricultural, industrial word picturing a process that is done until one finds the answer, the fruit, the product.

> Illustration: It can be likened to the process a gold miner would impose upon himself as a means of finding the best location for gold. He will work through the grid, marking the areas in which his soil samples indicate the greatest probability for gold, and focus on that area. That area becomes his 'work out' area.

Considering the theme of Philippians being that of joy, the minor now sees the newly labeled work space with joy on account of the potential yield coming from that area.

Have you followed thus far? Our theme of having a gospel that produces joy, is understanding that joy is not necessarily the product of being saved, but the stewardship of putting salvation to work, of utilizing grace. God is working our salvation. Living the gospel is a daily use of the grace which has been bestowed upon us when we were saved; joy is the product of claiming ownership of what God brings into our lives and witnessing the grace of God working through those situations, which lovingly wean us from the world and cause us to see an eternal way of life. This brings joy.

Working out our salvation is doing our part to implement sanctification, which is sponsored by grace. This includes human effort (i.e. bringing my body in subjection, this one thing I do). The issue is not a pietistic view— my growth is all up to me— or a quietist view—my growth is all up to God.

The issue is an obedience issue because of the grace given by God, which produces a joy as one of the wonders of salvation.

What we are to do? *You work out your own salvation.*

How are we to do it?
v. 13 For it is God which worketh in you...

We work out our salvation by being providentially reminded that He is God; by means of God giving us His thoughts when we read His Word; by means of His presence during one's Bible time, or the Spirit working through a particular sermon; by means of yielding to situations of life as growth opportunities, thus gaining the spirit "to will and to do of his good pleasure."

"For it is God which worketh in you" is a phenomenal opportunity "to will and do of his good pleasure." In fact, it is the only way to bring about biblical obedience, the one marking which causes humans to be able "to shine as lights in this crooked and perverse world."

Why are we to do it?
v. 11, 15, 18

Are we just going to talk about grace—God working in us—or are we going to utilize the power of grace?

So we could close with a statement and or a question and reveal the truths within the paragraph of Phil. 2:12-18.
- Why don't you grow up? Because you don't work out your salvation with fear and trembling
- Why you don't grow up: because you don't allow the grace of God to bring to surface the blessings and power of the gospel.

Selflessness—the Mark of True Leadership

Philippians 2:19-30 | Mark Herbster

19 But I trust in the Lord Jesus to send Timotheus shortly unto you, that I also may be of good comfort, when I know your state. 20 For I have no man likeminded, who will naturally care for your state. 21 For all seek their own, not the things which are Jesus Christ's. 22 But ye know the proof of him, that, as a son with the father, he hath served with me in the gospel. 23 Him therefore I hope to send presently, so soon as I shall see how it will go with me. 24 But I trust in the Lord that I also myself shall come shortly. 25 Yet I supposed it necessary to send to you Epaphroditus, my brother, and companion in labour, and fellowsoldier, but your messenger, and he that ministered to my wants. 26 For he longed after you all, and was full of heaviness, because that ye had heard that he had been sick. 27 For indeed he was sick nigh unto death: but God had mercy on him; and not on him only, but on me also, lest I should have sorrow upon sorrow. 28 I sent him therefore the more carefully, that, when ye see him again, ye may rejoice, and that I may be the less sorrowful. 29 Receive him therefore in the Lord with all gladness; and hold such in reputation: 30 Because for the work of Christ he was nigh unto death, not regarding his life, to supply your lack of service toward me.

Introduction

The theme of this chapter is that life should be lived for others. The theme continues all the way to the end of the chapter because not only do we have a heavenly example of Someone Who is selfless—the greatest sacrifice was that Jesus left heaven and He gave Himself for us; He humbled Himself and became a servant—but we also have, as Paul had, human examples of people who were selfless.

Everyone is a leader. Leadership is influence, and everyone is influencing someone. In this text, we have three levels of leadership: an apostle, a disciple of the apostle, and a layman in the church of Philippi.

I remember many years ago when I graduated from Tri-City Christian School in Kansas City, Missouri, in my graduation speech I commended three people who influenced me. Each of them had different leadership opportunities. The first person was my youth pastor who I commended for his faithful, selfless service to me. He was a man who reached out to me and built a relationship with me.

The second person was my coach, who coached me all the way through high school and was a very important influence on my life. And finally, I mentioned a person who is sitting in this room today here at MBU—Dr. Dave Brown who was a huge influence on my life as my choir and band director, and as my trumpet teacher; we spent a lot of time together.

As I was studying through this text, I was reminded of the people who have had influence in my life. And the common characteristic between them is selflessness.

One of the key verses in this text is verse 21: "For all seek their own, not the things which are Jesus Christ's." What a sad commentary. Paul is probably referring to many of the pastors and teachers and Christians he was with. We see that some of them in chapter 1 were preaching out of envy and strife; they were ministering for their own good.

What does it mean to be selfless? It is *a quality, a value, a virtue of life which causes us to care more about what other people need and want than about what we ourselves need and want.* Life should not be about you; life should not be about me. Life should be about touching the lives of other people.

Do you realize this quality of selflessness is recognized even in the business world?

> Great leaders are selfless; they are servants who facilitate the success of others. They spark action in others by seeing the value of others and aligning that value with a worthy cause. In the presence of great leadership, people feel inspired, not only in the worthiness of the cause that the leader is leading in, but in their own personal worth.[28]

Here is the theme of the message this morning: *Every Christian should seek to be a selfless leader.* In this text we see three profiles of selfless

---

[28] Robert Tanner, https://managementisajourney.com/in-100-words-or-less-the-selfless-leader/

leadership. The first one is the Apostle Paul, the second one is Timothy, and third one is Epaphroditus.

Profile Number One: Paul the Trusting Servant.

Paul was greatly used of God to influence other people, but it is clear in this text that one of the primary characteristics of Paul was that he cared about others. We see that he was a selfless, sacrificial leader in three ways:

A) Paul trusts in God. (v. 19, 24, 27)

"Trust" here is the Greek work for "hope." "I hope in the Lord." Notice verse 24: But I trust in the Lord. This is a different Greek word; it is the one for confidence in the Lord. You also can't miss his trust in the sovereignty of God in verse 27: But God had mercy on him. Paul recognized that God had his hand on Epaphroditus even in his sickness. One of the characteristics of a selfless leader, a trusting servant, is that they are resting and depending on the sovereign plan of God for their life (Prov. 3:5-6; Ps 37:5; Ps. 118:8; Prov. 29:25; Isa. 26:3-4).

B) Paul talks well of others. (v. 19-22; 25)

Here the Apostle Paul places himself on the same level as a student of his—a disciple of his—and also a convert in the local church. He recognizes the value and the virtues of these men.

One person said it this way, "When Paul was writing about other people, he would usually comment about four different things. First of all, he would comment about their work. He would recognize their work. Secondly, he would esteem, or honor, them in the specific situation because of their character and because of their consistency. Thirdly, he would usually comment on the relationship that he had with that person. And fourthly, he would lift up their significance."[29]

---

[29] O'Brien, P. T., *The Epistle to the Philippians: A Commentary on the Greek Text* (Grand Rapids, MI: Eerdmans, 1991), 329.

This is a powerful lesson for selfless leadership: we should recognize the gifts of other people and recognize the value of other people. And it is clear in this text that Timothy was very important to Paul. He was not only important to the Philippians, he was important to Paul. Paul valued Epaphroditus. How are we communicating about the people who are in our lives, whether they are over us or whether they are people who are under our leadership, that they are valuable?

Question: does the Bible say anything about our language about others? Sad to say, some people become known as critics, gossips, and slanderers instead of people who are building and edifying and lifting up the saints. Proverbs 10:18 says, "He that uttereth slander is a fool." Be careful! If you are a person who is constantly critiquing and complaining and criticizing and gossiping about other people, the Bible says you are foolish. If you utter slander, you are a fool. Psalm 101:5, "Whoso privily slandereth his neighbor, him will I cut off." So we should not speak evil of one another (James 4:11). And yet in Ephesians 4:29 the Bible says, "Let no corrupt communication proceed out of thy mouth, but that which is good to the use of edifying." This is the kind of speech that Paul the Apostle models in speaking of two of his friends. And we don't just see it here, we see it in every one of his epistles. Look at how he trusts God. Listen to how he talks about other people and notice how he treasures the ministry.

C) Paul treasures the ministry.

Paul longed for the church; he longed to be with Timothy and Epaphroditus. He wanted Epaphroditus to stay there with him, but he knew it was better for the church and better for Epaphroditus to send him back. And yet you just sense his love for the ministry, his love to help people, and his love to be selfless in his service.

Do you trust God's sovereign plan for you? How are you talking about other people? Do you have a passion for ministry? Do you love serving other people? This is the spirit that we see in this first profile: the Apostle Paul—the trusting servant.

Profile Number Two: Timothy—the Trusted Student.

Timothy had most likely been with Paul for ten years by the time of this writing. Throughout the New Testament, Paul describes Timothy: "my true son in the faith" (1 Tim. 1:2); "my beloved son" (2 Tim. 1:2); "my beloved and faithful son in the Lord" (1 Cor. 4:17); "my fellow worker" (Rom. 16:21); "our brother, fellow bondservant" (Phi. 1:1). There's an obvious love and concern for this trusted servant of Paul's.

Paul trusted Timothy so much that Paul depended on him as a co-laborer and representative frequently. Paul poured his life into Timothy; he trained him; he taught him. And yet Timothy also exemplifies for us what it means to care about others.

A) Timothy is "likeminded" with his leader. (v. 20)

This word "likeminded" is only used here in the NT. It is a compound adjective from two words which mean "equal" and "soul." It literally means "equal-souled." There was unity; there was like-mindedness as he was serving his leader.

We need to strive for like-mindedness with the people that are leading in our lives. I Peter 3:8 says, "Finally, be ye all of one mind, having compassion one of another." 2 Tim. 2:24, "And the servant of the Lord must not strive [don't be difficult; don't cause division; don't cause disunity], but be gentle unto all men...and patient." This is how Timothy was. No wonder Paul wanted to be with him. No wonder they had such a close relationship; they were likeminded. They were unified.

B) Timothy is loving to the church. (v. 20)

Selflessness is shown in the context of the local church. The church at Philippi was a very important church to Paul, and it became a very important church to Timothy. It was the only church that ministered to Paul in a financial way by sending the gifts with Epaphroditus. They had a special affinity for Paul, and Paul had a special love and friendship with them. And it was passed on to Timothy. No one else cared about the church like Timothy did. And Paul said that Timothy was the one he was going to send because he loved them! John 13:35 says, "By this shall all men know that ye are my disciples, if ye have love one to another." This is the characteristic of selfless leadership: that we care and we love other people, and specifically, we love brothers and sisters in Christ. I Thess. 3:12, "And the Lord make you to increase and abound in love one toward another and toward all men." Are you generating a love and a concern and a kindness for others?

    c)   Timothy is loyal to the gospel. (v. 22)

Paul says it this way: "He has served with me in the gospel." We know that Paul was not ashamed of the gospel. We know that Paul said in 1 Cor. 9:16, "Woe is unto me if I preach not the gospel!" But Paul adds this honor and commendation to Timothy by showing that Timothy's commitment was not only to his leader and not only to his church, but true selflessness is proved when you are committed to something higher and greater than the church and greater than the Apostle. True selflessness is proved when you are loyal to Jesus Christ. He was loyal to the gospel. And by God's grace, we will be as well.

Profile Number Three: Epaphroditus—the Trustworthy Steward.

Epaphroditus is a steward. In chapter 4 at the other occurrence of his name, Paul tells us that he was the one that was entrusted by the Philippian church to carry the gift to Paul.

His name comes from the Greek goddess Aphrodite, which literally means "to love." Epaphroditus means "lovely, charming, and amiable." And probably like Timothy, he was not a Jew; he was a Greek or Gentile believer who came to Christ in the church. Perhaps his family had been worshipers of the goddess and were converted when he was already bearing this name. It is a different name than the name that is mentioned in Col. 1:4—Epaphras. Epaphroditus exemplifies for us the spirit of sacrifice for the sake of the church and the sake of the gospel.

Notice the five terms that are mentioned here:

    A)   *My brother*. Paul and Epaphroditus had a tight connection; there was a relationship there; there was an affection for each other.

    B)   *Companion in labor*. This is a term which refers to laboring together, which Paul uses regularly in the New Testament to describe the people that join with him in the laboring of the gospel.

C) *Fellow soldier.* This is a military term to describe those who would fight side by side with each other. It obviously is speaking of his perseverance and his dedication to the gospel. Most likely he had persevered alongside of Paul in a lot of difficulties. One of the difficulties is expressed in this text: he was sick. Here he was with Paul in prison, and Epaphroditus was brought "nigh unto death" with some type of illness. And yet he persevered through that. He still brought the gift; he still was ministering to Paul. And it is interesting to note that his concern in this text is not about himself or his own illness, but his great concern was the fact that other people were anxious about his illness. Have you ever been around somebody like that? Who, while they were suffering, their great concern was that you wouldn't be concerned about them, but that you would be at peace? I have been around many situations like that, and that shows the selflessness that we need.

D) *Messenger.* Of course, a messenger is someone who is a delegate or a representative of Christ—one who is bringing a message. It is literally the word "apostle" here, but he was not an apostle in the same sense that Paul was. The word "apostle" is also one used to describe a general messenger of the truth or sometimes a group of messengers. And Paul sometimes used that term in that sense.

E) *Minister.* We get the word "liturgy" from this Greek word. It was used by the ancient Greeks to denote a public official who was passionate about the duties that he was to accomplish.

All of these terms show us that Epaphroditus is a great example for us. Would anyone in your life describe you this way? Are you a brother; a companion in labor; a fellow soldier; a messenger; a minister? These are all great terms that I hope someone would use to describe you. I hope someone might say this about me. Because these are terms that describe the selflessness of this man Epaphroditus.

So, what we're learning is that every Christian needs to be selfless. Because selflessness is the mark of true leadership. It is not how many you dominate; it is how many you serve. It is not who you are over; it is how many you are serving. It is how you are lowering yourself to become the kind of influence you should be. And this should be evidenced in our lives: that we are selfless in our leadership.

As I conclude today, I want to read to you from *Disciplines of a Godly Man*. The application is for both men and women here today. Kent Hughes has a chapter in his book called "Disciplines of Ministry." And in this chapter, he categorizes for us the two options that we have hearing a message like this. He says,

> "For people who claim the name of Christ, there are two distinct courses of life available. One is to cultivate a small heart for people. This by far seems the safest way to go about our lives because it minimizes the sorrows of life. If our ambition is to dodge the troubles of human existence, the formula is simple: avoid entangling yourself in any relationships, and do not give yourself to others. That's a really safe way to go. The second path is to cultivate a ministering heart. Open yourself to others, and you will become susceptible to an index of sorrows scarcely imaginable to the shriveled heart. No one has ever cultivated a ministry heart and lived to tell of a life of ease."

So, if you're looking for a life of ease, don't branch out. And here's how he concludes: he says,

> Little hearts, though safe and protected, never contribute anything. No one benefits from their restricted sympathies and vision. And yet, on the other hand, hearts that have embraced the disciplines of ministry [selfless ministry for others], though they are very vulnerable, those are the hearts which possess the most joy. And they leave their imprint on the world.

Shriveled heart—all about me. Open heart of ministry—all about others. And that's really the difference between a life of misery and a life of gospel-fueled joy. Selflessness. I think this is appropriate at this time in the semester, when we could become so self-focused that, literally, we could go day after day and think about no one except ourselves. I encourage you today to follow this example, because every Christian should be a selfless leader.

49

Taking Account of Life

Philippians 3:1-11 | Dr. Marty Marriott

Finally, my brethren, rejoice in the Lord. To write the same things to you, to me indeed is not grievous, but for you it is safe.² Beware of dogs, beware of evil workers, beware of the concision.³ For we are the circumcision, which worship God in the spirit, and rejoice in Christ Jesus, and have no confidence in the flesh. ⁴ Though I might also have confidence in the flesh. If any other man thinketh that he hath whereof he might trust in the flesh, I more:⁵ Circumcised the eighth day, of the stock of Israel, of the tribe of Benjamin, an Hebrew of the Hebrews; as touching the law, a Pharisee;⁶ Concerning zeal, persecuting the church; touching the righteousness which is in the law, blameless.⁷ But what things were gain to me, those I counted loss for Christ.⁸ Yea doubtless, and I count all things but loss for the excellency of the knowledge of Christ Jesus my Lord: for whom I have suffered the loss of all things, and do count them but dung, that I may win Christ,⁹ And be found in him, not having mine own righteousness, which is of the law, but that which is through the faith of Christ, the righteousness which is of God by faith: ¹⁰ That I may know him, and the power of his resurrection, and the fellowship of his sufferings, being made conformable unto his death; ¹¹ If by any means I might attain unto the resurrection of the dead.

Introduction

Windows 3.0 was introduced in May of 1990 with much anticipation. For months prior, I was recommending investing everything in Microsoft. My friend and broker listened politely but he thought Microsoft already had its run. MS had gone public in 1986 and experienced tremendous growth indeed. However, an investment of $100 in 1989 would be worth $50000 today. It's gone up 50000% since 1989. If I had invested my available funds, it would be worth many millions of dollars today.

What a missed opportunity! Yet, it's not a tragedy. But, to hold on to worldly values and to fail to invest in Jesus Christ is to be eternally destitute. That would be true tragedy.

The Bible teaches that Satan is a master counterfeiter, trying to pass off on unsuspecting people a version of Christianity that looks pretty good, but it is not going to be accepted by the bank of heaven. It's traumatic to get stuck with a counterfeit bill; but it would be far more traumatic to stand before God someday and hear Him declare that your Christianity is counterfeit!

As a believer, I want to invest in things that matter, in what will bring rejoicing now and forever. I want my life to be a lasting investment by living for the glory of God – for Jesus Christ and His gospel. I want to win Christ, to be found in His righteousness, and to know Him more fully – His power, fellowship and His life-giving death!

Rejoicing in Jesus is a Command.
vv. 1-2 Finally brethren, rejoice in the Lord...

To rejoice or glory in Jesus as God and Savior is the purpose of life. We were created for His glory. Here, as in 4:4, rejoicing is a command. The desire and capacity to rejoice in Jesus is a sign of being genuine (2:18).

The capacity to "rejoice in the Lord" (3:1) along with the three phrases in 3:3 characterize true followers of Christ – "worship in the spirit or Spirit of God," "glory or rejoice in Christ Jesus," and "have no confidence in the flesh." Test yourself by this measure: True Christians rejoice in the Lord. Do you?

A) Beware: There is a counterfeit Christianity and it takes many different forms.

Paul is speaking about one of the earliest counterfeits. Soon after the gospel came to the Gentiles, some Jews who claimed to believe in Christ began teaching the Gentile converts that they could not be saved unless they also were circumcised according to the law of Moses (Acts 15:1). They did not deny that a person must believe in the Lord Jesus Christ, but they added the keeping of the Jewish law to faith in Christ. The issue was debated and resolved in Jerusalem at a council of the church leaders (Acts 15:5-11).

Paul is warning the Philippian church about these Judaizers. The three terms in 3:2, "dogs, evil workers, and the concision," or mutilators performing false circumcision, all refer to one group, the Judaizers; theirs was a counterfeit Christianity. True Christians have put off all confidence in human merit and have trusted in Christ alone for salvation. The names

51

Paul calls these false teachers reveal three common forms such human merit takes:

1. One counterfeit puts faith in racial or ethnic status. Paul sarcastically calls these Judaizers "dogs." God chose the nation of Israel as His people and still has a special purpose for the Jews, but He is no respecter of persons when it comes to granting salvation through Jesus (Acts 10:34, 43; Rom. 10:12-13).

2. Another counterfeit is to put confidence in human works to please God.

Paul calls these men, who prided themselves on their good works, "evil workers." The Bible is clear that those who are saved by grace through faith apart from any works, will live a life of good works (Eph. 2:8-10; James 2:14-26). But the order of faith and works is essential!

3. Another religious counterfeit is to trust in religious rituals to gain a right standing with God.

Paul uses a play on words to call these men "the false circumcision." In Greek, circumcision is *peritome*; Paul calls these men *katatome*, which means "mutilators." There are many who mistakenly think that religious rituals such will get them into heaven.

B) Genuine Christianity relies totally on the person and work of Jesus Christ for salvation.

Although it is difficult to identify "the same things" (v. 1), there are two main interpretations: 1) it refers to the repeated theme of rejoicing, or 2) it refers to the repeated warnings about false teachers.

Paul may be referring to his emphasis on rejoicing. He has mentioned "rejoicing" repeatedly (1:18 twice, 2:17 twice, 18 twice, 28 once) and "joy" a total of eleven times (1:4, 25; 2:2, 29) in chapters one and two! Rejoicing in the Lord is the great antidote to rejoicing in self-reliance or achievement. It takes our focus off ourselves, it humbles our pride, and it focuses our faith when we rejoice in the Lord.

Paul is writing from prison as a result of confronting false religion. It seems that he is referring to his circumstances in comparison to those of the Philippians. To write to them is neither wearisome nor is it adding to Paul's suffering or persecution while in bonds, and the Philippians are receiving the message without fear of persecution – in fact this warning will make them safe from false teaching!

Rejoicing in Jesus is an Identifier of True Believers.
vv. 3-6

Because men and women are self-absorbed and self-focused, they are easily attracted to religion, rituals, good works and other forms of human effort. They often follow counterfeits with sincerity. But all the sincerity in the world is fatal if it is not in line with the truth. True Christianity is not just a matter of the head, but also of the heart. It is built on sound doctrine which is grasped by the intellect. But, if it stops there, you are not a true Christian.

A true Christian rejoices in the inner person. It is a matter of God changing our hearts, so that we rejoice in Him. But, verse 3 expands this description.

A)   Three characteristics of a person rejoicing in Jesus.

1.   He or she worships in the spirit or perhaps the Spirit of God (Jn. 4:24)

The false teachers were making worship a matter of outward ritual. Paul is saying that true Christians are marked by inner worship prompted by the indwelling Holy Spirit. True worship is offered in the domain of the spirit, not in the realm of external ceremonies.

2.   True Christianity is marked by "rejoicing or glorying in Christ Jesus."

The word is different than in verse one. It means "boast" or "glory." This word "boast" is one of Paul's favorite words, used some thirty-five times in his letters. True Christians are great boasters in Jesus Christ as the great Savior!

3.   True believers are those marked by "no confidence in the flesh."

The "flesh" is used to refer to *external ceremonies.*

Counterfeit Christianity builds a person's self-esteem: "You're great, you're worthy, and you're somebody!" True Christianity humbles all pride and confidence in self (Jer. 17:5)

B)   The example of Saul (4-6).

If ever there was a person who could be right with God by keeping the Jewish law, it was Paul himself. He had the credentials by birth; he had the track-record by experience. Every person who is truly converted will know that there is no place for human goodness of any kind as the basis of his or her justification.

Paul's list contains qualities which he formerly trusted in for right standing with God, but which he had written off as loss rather than gain.

- Inherited privileges (5a) *Circumcised the eighth day, of the stock of Israel, of the tribe of Benjamin, an Hebrew of the Hebrews*

- Personal attainments (5b-6) *as touching the law, a Pharisee; Concerning zeal, persecuting the church; touching the righteousness which is in the law, blameless.*

- Pharisee - Acts 23:6

- Persecutor - Acts 9:20-21; Acts 22:19-20

Rejoicing in Jesus is the Goal of Life.
vv. 7-11

The word 'count' is used three times in verses 7 and 8. Paul is saying, his profits were really losses. The supreme value of knowing Christ exceeds all other gains.

A)   To reach the goal demands loss.

Lightfoot brings out the nuance of the Greek text of verse 7: "All such things which I used to count up as distinct items with a miserly greed and reckon to my credit--these I have massed together under one general head as loss"[30].

Verses 8-11 consist of one complicated sentence. In verse 8 Paul not only calls his former credits a loss, but garbage. The word was used for excrement, human remains – half eaten dead body, food that has gone bad and scraps swept up from the floor[31]. We write off human effort for salvation and we must continue to write off all human merit as loss as we walk with Christ. True Christians count all human merit as loss.

    B)   To reach the goal is gain.

He suffered the loss of all things to win Christ! Paul expresses the same idea over and over here so that we don't miss it: he counted all things as loss
- "for Christ" (3:7);
- "for the excellency of the knowledge of Christ Jesus my Lord" (3:8);
- "that I may win Christ" (3:8);
- that I "may be found in Him" (3:9);
- "that I may know Him" (3:10).

What does it mean to gain Christ?

1. To gain the Lord Jesus Christ means coming to a personal knowledge of Him.

He says, "Christ Jesus *my* Lord" (3:8). There are no group or family salvation plans!

2. To gain the Lord Jesus Christ means a positional identification with all that He is.

---

[30] *Saint Paul's Epistle to the Philippians*, Zondervan, 148

[31] See Strong on 'dung'

To be found in Him is the only way to be right with God; it is to receive the righteousness that comes from God through faith.

This is *literally the 'through faith in Christ righteousness'* and is exactly opposite of Paul's former life and pursuit of righteousness. Faith is not something we must work up; faith is simply receiving what God has promised. It all happens at that instant, but Paul continues counting all his former merits as garbage. He continues to live by the same disposition.

C) The goal is summarized as knowing Christ.

The apostle Paul sums up the goal of the Christian life; it is to know Christ and to be like Him (v.10-11). The goal is to know Christ intimately. Jesus said the same thing when He prayed in John 17:3.

As with all relationships, it begins with an initial meeting or introduction (Acts 9:3-5a). It's the same with your relationship with Jesus Christ. If you are truly a Christian, you know Jesus Christ personally. You don't just know about Him; you know Him. You can say with Paul that He is "Christ Jesus my Lord."

Like any relationship, once you've met, you must cultivate that relationship. If you meet the guy or girl of your dreams, you must spend time together, getting to know one another through conversation and shared experiences. Verses 10 and 11 show the components and direction of the life of knowing Christ.

1. To know Christ requires knowing the power of His resurrection.

This is to know His power for living (2 Cor. 4:7). We do not live by our own power. That same resurrection power is necessary to sustain the believer as he walks in victory over sin.

2. To know Christ requires knowing the fellowship of His sufferings.

There is a sense in which we can never be like Him if we do not go through suffering and learn to entrust our souls to a faithful Creator in doing what is right (1 Pet. 4:19; Rom. 8:17-25). *Fellowship* points to closeness or intimacy. Those who suffer because of their faith in Christ know a special intimacy with Him. Paul knew this fellowship. When he

56

was preaching in corrupt Corinth, he was afraid, but the Lord appeared to him in a vision and promised to be with Paul (Acts 18:9-10).

3. To know and be like Christ requires being conformed to His death.

The goal is to be perfected by Him through experiencing His sufferings and dying to selfishness (Gal. 2:20). This is what Jesus meant when He said that whosoever follows Him must deny himself and take up his cross daily (Luke 9:23).

4. Christlikeness will be realized in the resurrection of the dead (11).

Verses 10-11 set the goal before us as that of Christ-likeness and the reward of the resurrection. Quite possibly the idea is that of *spiritual standing or rewards in the resurrection.* Or, 'if by any means' or 'somehow' might refer to either through death or Rapture.

But whatever this verse means, other verses make it clear that the process of sanctification will be completed. We will be like Him, totally apart from sin, sharing in His glory throughout eternity. This investment will pay off – now and forever – when I attain to the resurrection of the dead (v. 11; Isa. 51:6)

The goal of the perfected state, of final righteousness and complete, unbroken eternal fellowship with God has always been the longing of the redeemed (Ps. 17:15).

We rejoice:
- In new values and affections (3:3)
- In deliverance from empty rituals and self-effort (3:4-6)
- In loss of treasured garbage (3:7-8)
- In knowing Christ as Lord (3:8)
- In having a true righteous standing for faith in Christ (3:9)
- In knowing Him more (3:10)
- In experiencing His power (3:10)
- In the partnership of His suffering and death (3:10)
- In the assurance of His eternal reward (3:11)

Two Take-aways

1. 'No confidence in the flesh' is a disposition necessary for conversion, sanctification, and fruitful service (Gal. 3:3; John 15:5).

2. Counting losses and gains is necessary for intimate fellowship with Jesus Christ and the resulting eternal rewards.

- I count the loss of friends and popularity as gain if it is the result of godly decisions.
- I count the loss of wealth as gain if it maintains my integrity.
- I count the loss of health as gain, if it results in grace and power.

Gospel-Fueled Joy that Apprehends Grace

Philippians 3:12-16 | Dr. Steve Love

[12] Not as though I had already attained, either were already perfect: but I follow after, if that I may apprehend that for which also I am apprehended of Christ Jesus. [13] Brethren, I count not myself to have apprehended: but this one thing I do, forgetting those things which are behind, and reaching forth unto those things which are before, [14] I press toward the mark for the prize of the high calling of God in Christ Jesus. [15] Let us therefore, as many as be perfect, be thus minded: and if in any thing ye be otherwise minded, God shall reveal even this unto you. [16] Nevertheless, whereto we have already attained, let us walk by the same rule, let us mind the same thing.

This paragraph teaches two major truths:

- Spiritual perfection does not happen this side of heaven because the passage states *—have not already attained.*
- Personal spiritual growth is a must this side of heaven because the passage states *—I press toward the mark.*

Therefore, somewhere between these two bookends comes the impetus of this passage.

The Required Awareness
v. 12 Not as though I had already attained either were already perfect

This may sound elementary, but people who think they've arrived start living like they have arrived. People who think they've arrived are done moving forward. A required awareness for each believer is that salvation is not the end of the journey, but the beginning of the sanctification process, and if we live with a view that is opposite of such, we live in a way that has not been apprehended by grace.

I've heard it said, "We will never be more saved than we are now, but we should ever be examples that we are saved now." Salvation by grace assures the believers that they can never be more saved than they presently are. The wonderful truths of atonement, regeneration, and adoption guarantee such. But we must live if as if we have been apprehended by such truths. Atonement covers the problem of sin, regeneration cares for the matter of identity, and adoption encompasses the blessing of relationship. Surely with such in mind, one should live apprehending that for which they've been apprehended.

What apprehended Paul? What caught Paul? What seized him? All we have to do is look back to preceding paragraphs and we find that Paul had handfuls of things *he* had done, and now he wanted to seize things which *Christ* had done. He had been self-righteously filled with works, and now he wanted to be apprehended by grace. And be found in him, not having mine own righteousness, which is of the law, but that which is through the faith of Christ, the righteousness which is of God by faith (3:9).

The things, which Paul had apprehended prior to salvation, were now released and that same imagery overtook Paul in a newly found desire to be apprehended by Christ.

The Required Action
v. 12 I follow after … v. 13 I apprehend… v. 14 I press toward …

What we find in 3:12-16 is the opposite, and yet the same of what we find in 3:4-6; the difference is what we find in 3:9-10, which is what makes all the difference. Catch this—there is just as much focus on the word "I" in verses 4-6 as there is in verses 12-16. The human effort is just the same. In verses 4-6, which would be his unsaved condition, he lists what he (*I*) had accomplished by means of self-righteousness. In verses 12-16, which is his post salvation era, he lists what grace had accomplished. When we grasp the grace of the gospel, it is as if we are apprehended, or gripped by that grace. The other utilizes the word "I" to reveal what he had accomplished. Both reveal human effort but one was futile because it was not sponsored by grace.

A) The Inventory—v. 13

- Negative—*forgetting those things which are behind*—cutting loose those things, those non-grace efforts which so quickly make one look at self rather than at Christ and the abundant grace which He has given us.

60

- Positive—*reaching forth ... I press toward ... I follow after ... I may apprehend*
  In combined fashion these words epitomize the work of grace versus the works of self. These words reveal what really happens when grace sponsors sanctification. The same grace which releases us from the power of hell should now drive us toward prioritizing heaven. That's what grace does. It doesn't just work in one direction, caring for the past, but also committing one toward the future.

And, it's said in such commonsense language as presented in 3:13 with the words of *behind* and *forth*; you can't go forward while going backward.

Listed below is a series of statements, which I have written in the margin of my Bible. They are pungent provoking thoughts which I have gleaned down through the years while listening to others preach from this passage. Though I no longer have the ability to share their origin, I include them because they open up the meaning of the passage:

- *Those, with their eyes fixed on the past, risk a severe collision with the future.*
- *Use the past as a springboard, and not as a sofa.*
- *Some men dream of worthy accomplishments, while others stay awake and do them.*
- *There are some Christians that can't be called pilgrims, because they never make any progress.*

Now, let's look at our use of grace.

B) The Initiative—*I apprehend that for which I am apprehended*

How are we doing in this category? How do the words "I apprehend, follow, press toward, attained" look next to my name? Do these words fit being in the same sentence where my name is the subject of the sentence?

The idea is of grasping or latching on to biblical truths which come my way by means of grace and blessings. Listen carefully, those grace blessings, which sound so innocuous, don't come cheaply; they come by means of the cross—a huge truth which apprehended Paul (3:10).

C) The Identification—*Let us therefore* (15-16)

Which group do you want to be identified with: the group in the first part of chapter 3 or the group in the later part of chapter 3? The key is actually found in what we do with the middle verses of 9-12. Is your behavior motivated by law, or do you yield to God, motivated by His grace?

When Spain led the world in the 15th century, their coins reflected their national arrogance and were inscribed with the following words, *Ne Plus Ultra*, which meant "nothing further," meaning that Spain was the ultimate in the world. After the discovery of the New World, they realized that they were not the end of the world, so they changed the inscription on their coinage to *Plus Ultra*, meaning, "more beyond."

Are we living as though having arrived or is there more beyond in our grace relationship with Christ?

Who Are You Following?

Philippians 3:17-21 | Dr. Andrew Hudson

[17]Brethren, be followers together of me, and mark them which walk so as ye have us for an ensample. [18](For many walk, of whom I have told you often, and now tell you even weeping, that they are the enemies of the cross of Christ: [19]Whose end is destruction, whose God is their belly, and whose glory is in their shame, who mind earthly things.) [20]For our conversation is in heaven; from whence also we look for the Saviour, the Lord Jesus Christ: [21]Who shall change our vile body, that it may be fashioned like unto his glorious body, according to the working whereby he is able even to subdue all things unto himself.

Introduction

To whom are you listening? Whose opinion do you care about most? Who are you following on social media? Who are your friends on Facebook? It is possible to follow or friend someone on social media in order to get information or understand someone. That is not what I am talking about. I am asking whose posts/tweets/etc. are most influential in your Christian life? Most people have some level of influence over others. Many today call that influence a platform. "Platform" has even become a verb. Make no mistake, there are many today who are using their platform to influence behavior. There are endless examples of celebrities and athletes who actively use their platform to influence behavior. Who is having the most success in platforming you?

The apostle Paul understood the power of others' influence in our Christian walk. That is why he commanded believers to follow the right example in Philippians 3:17. This command is expressed in two actions. First, Paul commands believers to be fellow followers of his example. He is not bragging about his lofty Christian life or claiming perfection. He is simply instructing believers to follow his example of following Christ (1 Cor. 11:1). Follow Paul when he is successfully following Christ. Second, Paul commands believers to "mark" those who walk the same way. To "mark" is to observe someone in order to contemplate their behavior. It is a serious consideration of their lifestyle, to recognize and follow when they live biblically. Paul presents both actions as continuous tasks. It is not an occasional pursuit nor is it optional. Following the right example is an important practice for the believer.

Paul identifies himself and the ones walking correctly as "examples" at the end of verse 17. This word conveys the idea of a model or pattern. Humans normally learn by example or model. When my Greek language students learn how to write Greek letters for the first time, they begin by observing and tracing the Greek letters. After learning from the pattern, they progress to writing letters on their own. Last summer when I needed to recharge the air conditioning in my daughter's car, I got out my phone and found a YouTube video. I followed the video as my example. In our world today, there are both good and bad examples. That is why following the right example is vital for a believer. The same was true in Paul's day. He identifies bad examples in Philippians 3:18-19 and good examples in 3:20-21. Notice that both of these sections begin with the word "for." The reason that we must follow Paul's example and mark those who walk correctly is because there are both bad and good examples. Believers are responsible for determining who is a good example and who is a bad example. We must follow the right examples in our Christian walk!

Description of Good and Bad Examples
v.18, 20

If we are going to follow the right examples, we need to identify who is a good example and who is a bad example. In order to do this, we need to understand Paul's description of these examples in Philippians 3. Once we understand the identity of a good and a bad example, we will be able to consciously follow the right example.

Paul begins his description of examples by using the status of "enemy" and the status of "citizen." These are both common ideas in the 1st century Roman world. An enemy was one who was fighting against a government of which they were not part. An enemy of the cross fights against the church of which he is not part. He is hostile to believers and the cross. He is trying to undermine the church and destroy the gospel. He is not neutral. He is opposed to the lifestyle that believers are commanded to live. He may be talented, charismatic, convincing, powerful, and influential, but he is not using his "platform" to support the Word of Life or the Christian walk. We should not be surprised when we see enemies of the cross today. There are many today who mock Christian values, attack Christian standards, and reduce Christ to just another man. These enemies, at times, may even claim to be Christians (Titus 1:16).

The word "conversation" in verse 20 refers to the lifestyle that is consistent with a citizen. The verb form of this word is found in Philippians 1:27, "only let your conversation be as it becometh the gospel of Christ." Citizenship in the 1st century Roman world was not about location. In fact, Philippi was a Roman colony because there was not enough room for all of the Roman citizens in Rome. Their citizenship was about allegiance to Rome and commitment to the Roman way of living. It would be appropriate to translate 3:20, "for our citizenship is in heaven." Paul is using the citizenship status to contrast the enemy status in verses 18-19. Citizens of heaven swear allegiance to the God of heaven and commit to live the "heavenly" way of living. The citizen of heaven is the good example that believers should follow - the one who promotes the gospel and lives the Christian life in a worthy manner, one who supports the church and prays for the will of God.

In order to follow the right examples, we must discern between bad examples who are enemies of the cross and good examples who are citizens of heaven. The choice of who to follow is rather obvious. But we at times follow the wrong example. The allure of the enemies of the cross is both strong and subtle. It appeals to our flesh. We can become lulled into thinking that enemies are not that much of a threat. But following their example can have very destructive results. That is why Paul warned believers about them. Consider again those you are following or friending on social media. Are they enemies of the cross or citizens of heaven? Identifying their status is a start to following the right example.

Paul provides further description of both enemies and citizens in this chapter and contrasts *four characteristics of the enemy and citizen.*

Their Allegiance

The first characteristic he contrasts is their allegiance.

Status	Enemy	Citizen
Allegiance	Earthly things	Heavenly things

Paul says that enemies "mind" earthly things. "To mind" is to be intent on or to argue someone's case. Enemies are focused on arguing for earthly things. Earthly things are contrasted with heavenly things in this passage. There is a way of thinking-a worldview-that is consistent with an unbeliever's mind. This worldview dominates how the lost world views all of life. It controls their interaction with other humans. It controls their view of works. It controls their use of money. It shapes their view of love and tolerance. It determines their view of government. It convinces them to fight against biblical truth, to suggest that biblical truth is not welcome in the public arena. An enemy of the cross is going to promote this secular worldview. He will sing about it. He will produce movies about it. He will use his platform to influence people to follow his secular worldview. Let me illustrate this. There have been several Christian student organizations on secular college campuses lately that have been banned. This is an example of an enemy promoting his worldview by silencing a biblical worldview.

Citizens on the other hand are intent on heavenly things. Paul is using 1st century Roman citizenship as his model here. We should not read our modern concept of citizenship into this verse. Paul is not referring to a place; he is referring to an allegiance. Philippi was a Roman colony full of Roman citizens. The Roman citizens there did not think of returning to their homeland-Rome. They were intent on staying in Philippi. Roman citizenship was not about a place. It was about an allegiance. The Roman citizens in Philippi swore allegiance to the Roman lifestyle. They lived by it. They promoted and defended it. It was the grid through which they structured their lives. Claiming citizenship in heaven is not a statement about going there. It is being intent on a lifestyle that is defined there. This heavenly lifestyle is revealed in the pages of Scripture. It produces a biblical worldview. A citizen of heaven will live this biblical lifestyle. He will promote and defend it. It will shape the way he eats, the way he sings, the way he works, what he views, what he reads, what entertainment he consumes, and how he treats other people. It will be the grid by which he structures his life.

As you consider those you are following/friending on social media, ask whether they are promoting a secular worldview (earthly) or a biblical worldview (heavenly). To what have they sworn allegiance? Are you following an enemy or a citizen of heaven?

Their Walk

The second characteristic Paul contrasts is their walk. Both enemies and citizens walk in a way that is consistent with their worldview.

Status	Enemy	Citizen
Allegiance	Earthly things	Heavenly things
Walk	Fleshly desires	Worthy of the gospel
	Shame of man	Glory of God

Paul describes the walk or lifestyle of the enemies with two clauses. First, he says their god is their belly. "God" is a reference to who or what controls or drives one's behavior. We are a slave to whatever master we obey. The master or god of enemies is their belly. The most likely meaning of the "belly" is the fleshly desires that are sourced in one's sin nature. This is the same sin nature that is the source of the secular worldview to which enemies have sworn allegiance. The desires that drive an enemy of the cross are things like power, influence, self-reliance, pleasure, and pride. This produces a lifestyle that is similar to what Paul records in Romans 1:29-31, "Being filled with all unrighteousness, fornication, wickedness, covetousness, maliciousness; full of envy, murder, debate, deceit, malignity; whisperers, Backbiters, haters of God, despiteful, proud, boasters, inventors of evil things, disobedient to parents, Without understanding, covenantbreakers, without natural affection, implacable, unmerciful." Paul argues against this lifestyle in Romans 13:13, "Let us walk honestly, as in the day; not in rioting and drunkenness, not in chambering and wantonness, not in strife and envying." As an example of this lifestyle, consider the prevalence of unmarried people cohabiting. As a result of their desire to satisfy lusts of their flesh they live together in a way that fights against the biblical teaching about marriage. Sometimes this lifestyle is less blatant. But any lifestyle driven by the flesh makes that person an enemy of the cross.

Second, Paul says the enemy's "glory is in their shame." There is a lifestyle that brings shame on a person. Enemies glory in that lifestyle that brings them shame. They brag about living in a way that brings them shame. But they don't realize the shame they bring on themselves. Their fellow enemies bolster them in their shameful lifestyle. It is not unusual to hear enemies boast about their drunken escapades or their sexually immoral exploits at the proverbial water cooler. It is common to observe enemies flaunting their bodies in an immodest way. Consider the celebration of immodesty and sexual immorality in many music videos today. Their peers at award shows praise them for their shameful behavior! Consider the student who brags about cheating his way through college. Enemies of the cross boast about living in a way that satisfies the lust of their flesh, a life for which they ought to feel shame.

In contrast to the enemy's lifestyle, Paul has repeatedly described the citizen's lifestyle in the first three chapters of Philippians. In Philippians 1:27, citizens are instructed to live a lifestyle that is worthy of the gospel (one spirit, one mind, striving together for the gospel). This is a lifestyle that is driven by the Word of God. We are to avoid seeking our own things but instead to seek the mind of Christ (2:4-5). We are to work out our own salvation with fear and trembling because God works in us (2:12-13). We are to put no confidence in the flesh but instead be found in Christ gaining a righteousness that is by faith (3:1-10). We are to strive for the goal for which we were apprehended by Christ (3:13-14). A citizen of heaven will live a lifestyle that is consistent with the Word of God. He will say, "For me to live is Christ!" He will boast in the cross of Jesus Christ rather than in shameful things.

A citizen will not revel in shameful things. Instead, he will pursue things that bring glory to God. In Philippians 2:14-16 Paul says we are to shine as lights in this dark world, holding fast to the Word of truth. The picture of shining as lights suggests we are living in a way that is consistent with truth. In doing that, we image God. We bring Him glory.

There is a clear difference between the lifestyle of the enemy and the lifestyle of the citizen. The enemy is driven by the flesh and boasts in shameful things. The citizen is driven by the Word and boasts in Christ. Which of these categories do those who influence you most on social media fit? We should evaluate them to be sure we are following the right examples.

Their Expectation

The third characteristic that Paul contrasts is expectation. The future holds radically different prospects for the future.

Status	Enemy	Citizen
Allegiance	Earthly things	Heavenly things
Walk	Fleshly desires	Worthy of the gospel
	Shame of man	Glory of God
Expectation	Destruction	Transformation

The enemies of the cross will have as their final end "destruction." Those who are driven by an earthly worldview and live according to their sin nature will meet destruction. Destruction is Paul's way of describing eternal damnation. Enemies might seem prosperous now. They might seem to be unencumbered by the judgment of God. But make no mistake. They will face eternal damnation in the end. Paul uses the same word in Philippians 1:28 when he argues that our fearless worthy Christian lifestyle is a sign to the enemies of their destruction. As believers live in a way that is consistent with their citizenship in heaven without any fear of the enemies, we are a living reminder to the enemies of their future eternal damnation. Paul continues in 1:29 to remind believers that it has been granted to us not only to believe but to suffer as well. Enduring suffering now at the hands of the enemies of the cross will remind them of their end—destruction. The enemies' destruction is certain. In 3:21 Paul assures believers that Jesus will subject all things to himself. There is no hope for the enemies to defeat Christ. Their greatest power is weakness in comparison to the power of Christ.

Because God uses the lifestyle of the citizens of heaven to remind enemies of their future eternal destruction, enemies will not react pleasantly to citizens. Enemies will encourage citizens to participate with them in their shameful activities. Enemies will ridicule citizens for their choice of standards and behaviors. Enemies will attempt to demonize citizens. In other words, enemies will do all they can to destroy the reminder of destruction. If enemies can get citizens to follow their shameful lifestyle, the reminder of their destruction is mitigated. Instead of placing their faith in Christ to escape eternal destruction, they press everyone around them to live like them, so they don't have to think about their destruction. Is your life an appropriate reminder of the enemies' eternal destruction?

Believers, on the other hand, are eagerly and confidently awaiting the Savior, the Lord Jesus Christ. When Jesus comes, He will transform our sin cursed corruptible bodies into bodies that are like His glorious resurrected body. Instead of facing destruction, the citizen of heaven will experience eternal life in a glorified body. Even though we suffer now at the hands of the enemies, our end will be quite different than the enemies' end. We will live forever on the new earth with the Lord in incorruptible bodies.

Paul is not giving a lesson in eschatology in this passage. He is not trying to distinguish between the rapture (when we will receive our glorified bodies) and the second coming of Christ (when we will live with Christ in the kingdom). Both of these elements are alluded to in 3:20-21. Paul is using an element of the citizenship model to assure believers of their glorious future with Christ. The Roman citizens in Philippi did not expect to return to Rome when life became difficult in Philippi. There was not enough room for them in Rome. They were not wanted in Rome. What Roman citizens in Philippi did rightly expect was a visit from the emperor. When there were significant problems in Philippi, the emperor would come and fix those problems. The emperor would make it possible to live life as a Roman citizen in Philippi without any resistance. Paul used this model to assure believers that Christ will come and fix things on earth so believers can live as citizens of heaven on earth without any resistance. This will become a reality in the future kingdom of the eternal state.

The believer who is a citizen of heaven has a glorious future. The enemy of the cross has a tragic future. Given this end, it is no wonder that Jesus said we should not fear the enemy of the cross. As you consider who you follow, keep in mind the end of those you are following. Are you following a winner or a loser?

Their Response

The fourth characteristic that Paul contrasts is the believer's response. Paul models the correct response believers ought to have for enemies. He also teaches the appropriate response for a believer who is living as a worthy citizen of heaven.

Status	Enemy	Citizen
Allegiance	Earthly things	Heavenly things
Walk	Fleshly desires Shame of man	Worthy of the gospel Glory of God
Expectation	Destruction	Transformation

Believer's Response	Weeping for the enemy	Rejoicing in Christ

Paul had often warned the believers about the enemies of the cross. He does so again in Philippians. This time he says that it causes him to weep. Some suggest that Paul is weeping for believers because he needs to instruct them about the false teachers again. If this was the case, it is likely that Paul would have included the concept of weeping in verse 17 where he is exhorting believers. Instead, Paul couches the fact that he is weeping in the middle of the description of the enemies of the cross. His grammar makes it clear his weeping is for the false teachers. Paul takes no joy in the focus or lifestyle or end of the enemies. He is weeping tears of sorrow for them. We should follow Paul's example of weeping for the enemies of the cross. We should take no joy in enemies.

There are four wrong responses that believers sometimes express regarding enemies of the cross.

- First, some ridicule them. This is often done to confirm our right position. We should never make fun of our enemies. We should feel genuine sadness for them.
- Second, some will rejoice over the demise of the enemies of the cross. I remember vividly a group of people (many Christians) standing outside the building in which a serial killer was facing the death penalty. When it was announced that he was executed the crowd began cheering and celebrating. I understand the satisfaction that justice brings. But it is wrong to cheer when an enemy dies and faces eternal damnation. Anytime a lost person faces the wrath of God, there should be a sense of sadness; a genuine weeping for them.
- Third, some will rejoice over the exploits of the enemies of the cross. When an enemy of the cross glories in what ought to bring shame, believers should not be there cheering them on. How many of the people we follow on social media are really enemies? Are you rejoicing in their exploits? We should be weeping.
- Fourth, some long for the things that the enemies have or do. If we are genuinely weeping for the enemy, why would we want what they have? Why would we want to do what they are doing? Paul commanded those who are genuine believers to seek those things that are above; not the things on the earth (Col. 3:1).

We should weep for the enemies of the cross. But how should we respond to citizens of heaven who are walking in a way that is worthy of the gospel? Paul does not tell us in Philippians 3:20-21. But he has already told us earlier in the epistle. It should bring us great joy to observe those who are walking as faithful citizens of heaven. Paul said as much in Philippians 2:2. He tells the Philippian believers that they would complete or fill up his joy if they walked in one mind, had the same love, were united in spirit, and had one purpose. In other words, it would bring Paul much joy if the Philippian believers lived as worthy citizens of heaven. In fact, joy or rejoicing is a frequent theme in Philippians.

Sometimes believers do not live a life that is worthy of the gospel. We should not find joy in disobedient believers. We should be sorrowful for them. Paul said his joy was full *when* believers lived as worthy citizens of heaven. Paul expresses no joy when urging Euodias and Syntyche to "be of the same mind" (Phil. 4:2-3). He enlists the help of others to encourage them back to a worthy Christian walk. There are times in life when disobedient believers close to us cause us much pain because they are following enemies of the cross rather than citizens of heaven. They will not face the same destruction as the lost, but they cause us sorrow, nonetheless. Only those who are walking as worthy citizens of heaven should fill us with joy.

How do you respond to those who are living worthy of the gospel? Unfortunately, we do not always rejoice. Sometimes we are plagued by envy or jealousy when we see God's blessing in the obedient life of other believers. Sometimes we are angry because they point out weaknesses in our own lives. Sometimes we ridicule them because we pursue a different lifestyle. None of these responses are biblical. We ought to rejoice when other believers are walking in truth. We ought to "mark" them and be fellow imitators with them.

Conclusion

We must follow the right examples in our Christian walk. There are two kinds of examples: enemies and citizens. Paul does not present a third neutral option. We are either rightly following a citizen of heaven or we are wrongly following an enemy of the cross. You can identify whether someone is a citizen or an enemy by their allegiance and walk. You know their end. You ought to weep for enemies and rejoice for citizens. Once you identify whether someone is an enemy or a citizen, you can choose to follow the right example. We must follow those who are walking as worthy citizens of heaven.

Application

Go back to your social media accounts. Look at who you are following. Which of your friends are most influential in your life? Who are you trying to be like the most? You are following the example of those who are most influential in your life.

1. Who has the most influence in your life?
2. Can you find any good examples of a citizen of heaven in your friend list?
3. Can you name one person who is a proper example for you?

Gospel-Fueled Joy in the Middle of Chaos

Philippians 4:1-9 | Dr. Bruce Meyer

Therefore, my brethren dearly beloved and longed for, my joy and crown, so stand fast in the Lord, my dearly beloved. ² I beseech Euodias, and beseech Syntyche, that they be of the same mind in the Lord. ³ And I intreat thee also, true yokefellow, help those women which laboured with me in the gospel, with Clement also, and with other my fellowlabourers, whose names are in the book of life. ⁴ Rejoice in the Lord always: and again I say, Rejoice. ⁵ Let your moderation be known unto all men. The Lord is at hand. ⁶ Be careful for nothing; but in every thing by prayer and supplication with thanksgiving let your requests be made known unto God. ⁷ And the peace of God, which passeth all understanding, shall keep your hearts and minds through Christ Jesus. ⁸ Finally, brethren, whatsoever things are true, whatsoever things are honest, whatsoever things are just, whatsoever things are pure, whatsoever things are lovely, whatsoever things are of good report; if there be any virtue, and if there be any praise, think on these things. ⁹ Those things, which ye have both learned, and received, and heard, and seen in me, do: and the God of peace shall be with you.

Introduction

The American College Health Association found in its annual survey in 2011, that 50 percent of undergraduates reported they felt "overwhelming anxiety." By 2017, the number had risen to 61 percent. Without question anxiety has risen substantially, perhaps under pressure from the instantaneous and steady stream of pessimistic news we receive through the internet. In the face of such anxiety, many turn to contemporary solutions only to be disappointed with the outcome. These contemporary solutions include prescription drugs, safe zones, essential oils, vaping, adult coloring books, alcohol, and the like.

Since I'm a man, I'm quite fascinated by gadgets. Two such gadgets surfaced as surprising "stress relievers" between the fall of 2016 and spring of 2017. While developers expected only modest sales, both devices surpassed sales expectations, returning millions in sales rather than mere thousands. The first was the Fidget Cube, grossing nearly $6.5 million in sales. This anxiety reliever was later eclipsed by the popularity of the Fidget Spinner. I'm curious how many of you own a fidget spinner? Some of you. I don't personally own one, but I'm still amazed by their popularity. On this, a Vox reporter stated, "We're not understanding how to deal with [mental health]. Instead, we're throwing products at it. It's very American."[32]

But chaotic and anxious times are nothing new. In the early church when Paul wrote this letter to his friends in Philippi, Paul was in prison and the Philippians were facing uncertainty about their future in light of his imprisonment. Through our study in Philippians, we have observed that the gospel fuels our joy. In an earlier sermon, we defined joy as "A Spirit enabled contentment with God and His will that restrains from sinful responses and is the mainspring of our satisfaction and happiness in life." But how do we maintain such joy in the face of such uncertainty and angst? How are we to maintain this kind of peaceful joy during the chaos we face in this world?

We have learned that Paul expresses his theme for this letter in Philippians 1:27, "Only let your conversation be as it becometh the gospel of Christ: that whether I come and see you, or else be absent, I may hear of your affairs, that ye *stand fast* [notice those words!] in one spirit, with one mind striving together for the faith of the gospel." Paul envisioned a unified body of believers, a theme that he carries throughout the book as he explains his perspective on his imprisonment and opportunities in the gospel (Ch. 1), joy in serving (Ch. 2), joy in knowing Christ (Ch. 3), and now, joy during difficult circumstances.

One of the unifying themes in our passage today is "peace." In the preceding context (3:17-21), Paul reminds his brothers and sisters that because our citizenship is in heaven, we are longing to see Jesus' return so that our lowly body can be transformed into his likeness. But notice what Paul commands in Philippians 4:1 "Therefore, my brethren dearly beloved and longed for, my joy and crown, so stand fast in the Lord, *my* dearly beloved."

---

[32]   https://www.vox.com/the-goods/2018/9/10/17826856/fidget-spinners-weighted-blankets-anxiety-products

In light of the truth of 3:20-21 concerning Jesus' return, Paul exhorts us to "stand fast" in the Lord, that is, to stand firm, hold our position. The "therefore" of verse 1 ties this passage to the previous. "Stand firm" is a military term that Paul uses to exhort us not panic in the face of hardships and uncertainties. But also note the love that Paul communicates in this instruction. He wants these believers to know that they're not alone in this battle, that he loves them, and cherishes their testimony. He uses the words, "brothers," "dearly beloved," "longed for," "joy and crown," and repeats "dearly beloved." Paul's affection for these believers communicates his concern for and association with these believers.

Paul writes this passage, therefore, to exhort believers to stand firm in chaotic times through our committed relationship to both Christ and His Word resulting in peace. Paul is calling us to be actively engaged in pursuing this peace through three exchanges.

Exchange Problems for Christ-Centered Unity
vv. 2-3

Now before we look at this truth, let me remind you that there are times in the Scriptures when God provides us with steps as he does here. But we must always remember that steps are based upon the relationship we have with Christ, a relationship which Paul most clearly defines in Philippians 3:8-10. Steps only work in relationship—steps by themselves can and do cater to the flesh. Steps in relationship to Christ become truths that are grace-based.

This first exchange seems out of place, but it's actually in keeping with what Paul has already taught in Philippians 2, that is to look on the needs of others above ourselves as patterned by the Lord Jesus (2:1-11). It is an exchange that fits the unity in the gospel theme that Paul has emphasized throughout this letter. Here, however, there is an obstacle to the unity in the church. There were two women who apparently had a disagreement over something unknown to, but it was a disagreement that was affecting the unity of the church. Why else would Paul mention by name two ladies, Euodias and Syntyche, to have them resolve their squabble? Can you imagine being these ladies, sitting in the assembly when this letter was first read? How embarrassing. But this step demonstrates how seriously Paul views a threat to unity as an obstacle to the church's well-being. Therefore, Paul calls them to "be of the same mind," to agree on whatever was dividing them so they too could be unified as sisters in Christ around the gospel.

To assist them, Paul calls upon an unnamed associate ("true companion") to assist these ladies in resolving their conflict (v. 3). Paul does commend these ladies for their co-laboring in the gospel along with him, so these are not the false teachers of 3:2. These are genuine servants in the gospel.

We learn two important principles from this section. First, our disagreements with other believers, either large or small, affect the unity of the church and the advancement of the gospel. Second, resolving problems greatly aids the church in its unity and growth in the gospel. Paul is wise to solve the problems he can solve. Paul doesn't attempt to solve what he cannot solve—he's in prison and there were people preaching in such a way to add to his affliction (Phil. 1:15-16). One author reminds us that "Genuine Christian joy is not inward-looking. It is not by concentrating on our need for happiness, but on the needs of others, that we learn to rejoice."[33] Paul was calling these two to manifest a servant's attitude towards each other to solve the problem.

So, I suspect in an audience this size that there are students who have a variety of problems, some of which we can solve. If you're expecting a difficult exam or paper, then the answer is to start preparing early and rigorously. If you wait until the night before or the day of, you haven't solved the problems you can solve. If there is a broken friendship, there is a solution to that. Fix what you can!

Paul, however, doesn't just deal with our actions—he also addresses our attitudes, because it is here that we often struggle the most, for our attitudes derive from our theology— our beliefs about God, ourselves, and the world around us. It is our attitude that often sets the course of our direction when in chaos. So, Paul instructs us to exchange problems for Christ-centered unity, and then, second, he teaches us to:

---

[33] Moises Silva, *Philippians,* BECNT (Grand Rapids MI: Baker, 2005)

Exchange Negative Attitudes for Christ-Centered Joy
vv. 4-5

This instruction helps us with the problems we can't change. Paul issues a command in this case to "rejoice in the Lord." We should notice right away that God is not calling us to rejoice in our circumstances. That would be foolish. If I fall on ice and fracture my arm, I'm not going to rejoice that I have a broken arm. Paul instead commands us to focus our rejoicing in the one possession we have that never changes, regardless of changing times or circumstances around us. Notice the words, "in the Lord." This is a constant rejoicing that we are to maintain. It is the vertical direction that alters our view of the horizontal circumstances. Remember Dr. Saxon's definition: "A Spirit enabled contentment with God and His will"? God is the object of this rejoicing. We're really talking here about worship—admiring God for who He is and what He has done. This focus changes our entire perspective on the circumstances that we face.

Oh, that's easy for Paul to say, right? Paul knows that such a rejoicing will not be easy for us, because he repeats this command twice. There are also three indications in this verse of the constancy of this command. He plainly says that we are to rejoice *always* but he also uses a present imperative in both clauses indicating that this attitude of rejoicing is to be constant in our lives.

It is important for us to distinguish between joy and happiness. Happiness is based on our circumstances—happenings! Joy is an attitude of worship, a rejoicing that is based on the very nature and character of God. My financial status, my grades, my health, my relationships, my safety, my good feelings—all of these can change in a moment. But God's nature and work don't change—they are both constant.

I frankly haven't felt much like smiling this year for various personal reasons. Mom's cancer and resulting death last year was a difficult time. I thought that would be the worst of my problems for the year, but our family has suffered an even bigger loss, one that has indescribably broken our hearts. But I know that God is with us through this time of hardship. I know that, because he has always been with us and he never fails, no matter how hard, painful, terrifying, or heartbreaking our circumstances.

So, this rejoicing is a constant attitude in the vertical sphere of my attitude towards God. When this vertical attitude is in place, it helps in adjusting my actions towards others, that is, the horizontal relationships. So, Paul addresses these relationships in verse 5, "Let your moderation be known unto all men. The Lord *is* at hand." The word "moderation" is the idea of a sweet reasonableness toward others. When we are in pain, have you noticed how easy it is to lash out at others in anger or harshness? Paul is teaching us that when we have that vertical attitude of rejoicing in place, then we can also be reasonable towards others.

This reasonableness demonstrates my belief that God is near. This theology drives me to reflect this truth in my life. Now, commentators disagree over what Paul means in this clause, "the Lord is at hand." Most believe that Paul is referencing *the return* of Jesus being near at hand. This interpretation is appealing because Paul typically is looking forward to the Lord's return. The preceding context in 3:20-21 supports this idea also. But I lean towards a more personal presence in this case, that is, the Lord is close by me in my suffering, my anxieties, and my fears. The reason I lean this direction is because in verse 9, Paul reminds us again that the "God of peace shall be with you." Either way, Paul wants us to remember that the Lord is near to us both personally ("I will never leave you nor forsake you" — Hebrews 13:5) and eschatologically (His return is near). Both truths overlap and provide the hope that bolsters me in a time of chaos. I demonstrate this theology to others when I treat them with grace in a time of suffering or hardship.

So, we solve the problems we can solve by exchanging problems for Christ-centered unity and we exchange negative attitudes for an attitude of rejoicing, focusing on both the vertical relationship with God and the horizontal with others. But at this point we can acknowledge that fear is still powerfully overwhelming when chaos strikes. So, is there teaching that Paul offers concerning the feelings I may have when overwhelmed? What do I do with those anxious thoughts and feelings I have when my circumstances are absolutely out of control? The third exchange that Paul commands is:

Exchange Anxiety for Christ-Centered Peace
vv. 6-8

Here, after having dealt with our attitudes, Paul now deals with our anxieties, both through our thoughts and our actions. So how does one who is living through chaotic circumstances find peace? Paul is very practical here. He teaches us that we are to replace our worry, fear, anxiety, (the word "careful" stresses our cares or anxieties) with a dependency upon God through prayer. Paul piles up words for prayers to stress our action of bringing those fears or concerns to God himself and he reminds us that we are to do this in "everything" (v. 6).

Paul even includes "thanksgiving" which we usually associate with an answer to prayer. It seems then that Paul is already expecting an answer to his prayers, so thankfulness is already a part of his response. This thankfulness reinforces the "rejoicing" that we saw in the previous verses. So, Paul calls us here to drive anxiety out of our lives with a trusting dependency upon God to meet our needs in chaotic circumstances.

My need might be for wisdom (James 1). My need might be for the intercessory work of Jesus (Hebrews 4). My need might be the support of the church (Romans 12). My need might be for abundant grace (2 Corinthians 12). God stands ready to supply as I ask for his help in times of chaos.

Paul not only provides the means of driving out worry, he also provides us with the results of this action. Here is a promise about God's peace. God's peace, even though it doesn't make sense (it "passes all understanding"), keeps or guards—a military term—our hearts and minds (v. 7). Paul often uses "hearts" and "minds" interchangeably, but here I wonder if he isn't emphasizing both our feelings ("hearts) and our thoughts ("minds"). At the very least, Paul is stressing that God's peace permeates our entire being to drive out the anxiety we may be feeling. This peace sets up a sentinel to guard us from the fear that impairs and destroys. The truth is we serve a God of peace who desires to hear and answer our needs.

Have you noticed that when we are in times of suffering, we often don't have answers? And even when we have some answers at times, we still may not understand the answers or the situation. And sometimes, we have answers, we understand them, and the situation still stings! That's why we need the peace of God through this active dependency in prayer. It is God's presence and work for us that give us assurance. One author reminds us that when we're in trouble, God doesn't always offer us solutions, but he offers us something even better—Himself!

The second action that Paul commands here is equally practical in helping us with our anxiety. Paul tells us the command at the end of verse 8—to "think on these things." What things? Paul piles up several words that describe the kinds of thoughts we are to think. Notice verse 8: whatever is true, honorable, right, pure, lovely, and admirable are the words that Paul uses. In short, these are thoughts that edify rather than destroy.

I've noticed that my worst time for worry is at night. I can awaken, or be half awake, and suddenly, without any warning, fall into worry so easily. For instance, I can notice that I have a small paper cut on my finger, a cut that I didn't even notice during the day. At night, that paper cut can grow to crisis-proportions quickly as my mind engages in worry. In short order, my paper cut can move from a simple cut to a massive laceration, to infection, to gangrene, to losing my finger, then my hand, then my life! A simple night time headache becomes a massive tumor or brain aneurysm or stroke. It's amazing how darkness can intensify our fears. All these afflictions are of course possible, but certainly not very likely, especially since I've never become critical because of a paper cut. This is more than just positive thinking however—this process is actually truth and honor and right and pure and lovely and admirable thinking. It's thinking God's thoughts rather than fear thoughts. It's looking at life through faith glasses rather than fear glasses. So, what does this replacement principle look like?

Paul loves this concept of replacement—he uses it often. Suppose I say to you now *not* to think about the color red—whatever you do, don't think about red! There are people seated around you who are wearing red. Avoid thinking about red even as you see that red scattered throughout the audience. The response usually is, "don't think about red; don't think about red!" The problem is when I'm thinking that way, I'm thinking about red! In other words, the person who is thinking about *not* worrying or *not* fearing, is still thinking about worry and fear. In the same way, the person who is thinking about not sinning is just as consumed with sin as the person who is thinking about sinning. God wants us to be thinking about Him, not our anxiety, fears, or sin, either to do sin or to resist sin. The answer to resisting temptation is to focus on God in our lives rather than the size of our sin struggles, the size of our fears, or the size of our circumstances. Therefore, I'm filling my mind with thoughts that edify after the grace and beauty of God rather than after the ugliness of my circumstances.

Conclusion

Paul has commanded us to hold our ground during difficult circumstances, to not panic. He has now provided us with three exchanges that we must make to stand firm—exchange problems for Christ-centered unity, exchange negative attitudes for Christ-centered joy, and exchange anxiety for Christ-centered peace. Our response might be, "Paul, you really don't understand my problems and the enormity of my anxiety. Paul doesn't live in the real world!" But let's consider when Paul penned these words, he was in prison, his future was uncertain, there were disagreements from within the church, and there were enemies from without. Paul is not writing these words in a vacuum, from what he wants to happen in the lives of others.

Think back with me for a moment when Paul first visited Philippi in Acts 16. He and Silas were arrested and then beaten without a trial. If that's not bad enough, they were put into a cell in stocks for the night. I doubt I could be at peace in a jail cell sitting in stocks. I can imagine myself grumbling and complaining—I serve God and *this* is what I get—beatings, a cold jail cell, and my hands and feet in stocks. But what were Paul and Silas doing at midnight? Complaining? Grumbling? Giving into fear and anxiety? Amazingly, they were singing hymns. Paul had experience with terrible circumstances. Read 2 Corinthians 11:23-28 sometime for a glimpse into his sufferings. But I want you to notice how Paul concludes this passage in Philippians 4:9, "Those things, which ye have both *learned*, and *received*, and *heard*, and <u>*seen in me!*</u>" Paul not only teaches these truths, but he lived them; he displayed them. The Philippians had seen—they were seeing—Paul practice them. They were seeing the peace of God that passes all understanding through Paul's life.

Now Paul says, these things, just "do" them! It's the *Nike* slogan—Just do it! Practice these truths and the "God of peace shall be with you."

You want God's peace? It doesn't come by positive thinking, by fidget spinners, alcohol, or denial. You might be facing health problems with either you or a family member. You might have a financial worry. You might be struggling with your grades. You might be suffering with an interpersonal conflict with someone you love. You might have a family member who has walked away from the Lord. Whatever your anxiety, you can have the peace of God by following these instructions as you walk with Christ.

Believers, stand firm in chaotic times through your committed relationship to Christ and commitment to His Word resulting in peace.

Financial Partnership in Ministry

Philippians 4:10-23 | Dr. Preston Mayes

[10] *But I rejoiced in the Lord greatly, that now at the last your care of me hath flourished again; wherein ye were also careful, but ye lacked opportunity.* [11] *Not that I speak in respect of want: for I have learned, in whatsoever state I am, therewith to be content.* [12] *I know both how to be abased, and I know how to abound: every where and in all things I am instructed both to be full and to be hungry, both to abound and to suffer need.* [13] *I can do all things through Christ which strengtheneth me.* [14] *Notwithstanding ye have well done, that ye did communicate with my affliction.* [15] *Now ye Philippians know also, that in the beginning of the gospel, when I departed from Macedonia, no church communicated with me as concerning giving and receiving, but ye only.* [16] *For even in Thessalonica ye sent once and again unto my necessity.* [17] *Not because I desire a gift: but I desire fruit that may abound to your account.* [18] *But I have all, and abound: I am full, having received of Epaphroditus the things which were sent from you, an odour of a sweet smell, a sacrifice acceptable, wellpleasing to God.* [19] *But my God shall supply all your need according to his riches in glory by Christ Jesus.* [20] *Now unto God and our Father be glory for ever and ever. Amen.* [21] *Salute every saint in Christ Jesus. The brethren which are with me greet you.* [22] *All the saints salute you, chiefly they that are of Caesar's household.* [23] *The grace of our Lord Jesus Christ be with you all. Amen.*

Introduction

Handling money well is like eating fruits and vegetables: everyone knows what they should do, but few do it. Sometimes financial struggles are beyond their control. Medical bills, job loss, or death of a spouse all create significant hardship. And of course, some believers have money and manage it well, both saving and giving generously. One suspects, however, that most church members fall into one of two categories. Some will be good with money but hoard it. Others will spend too much and struggle financially.

The effect of poor financial stewardship is immediately apparent in church ministries. Though we know that the Lord is not dependent on us and can accomplish his goals without us, he has chosen to use us. Financial support of ministry is a delicate topic. On the one hand, Scripture says much about money, including the duty of pastors to teach their people to manage it well. On the other hand, how does a pastor talk about stewardship without leaving the wrong impression? Raising the issue of money may seem self-serving. After all, the offerings pay the pastor's salary. And how should he even approach the topic given the range of financial situations in most churches? How will the charge to give be perceived?

Philippians 4:10-19 offers a helpful perspective on pastors, church members, and money. The text records Paul's thanks for those who have given sacrificially to support his ministry, and the text reflects a situation in which both minister and member have discharged their responsibilities well. So, what example should a pastor set to create the right climate for giving? How should I view money in general as a church member? A pastor will need to first model the right response to money, then lead his people to handle it well. Only by this two-pronged approach can people be led to view the use of their money as a God-given responsibility.

Leaders

Praise the Lord for those who consistently support ministry. It has been rightly stated that a person's checkbook—or in today's economy credit card statement—reflects his priorities. Often those priorities are self-centered. But the Philippian church had not been guilty of such. Paul begins by praising Christ greatly for the obvious signs of His work in their lives. That they were growing in their faith and eager to support the spread of the gospel was more important to Paul than the gift itself. And their faithfulness was indeed great. They had sent to Paul early in his ministry, and now they were doing so again. Their actions reflected a consistent and ongoing concern for him (as indicated by the verb tense). Ministry can be discouraging when there is no sign of growth. It is truly encouraging to see signs that the Lord is consistently working in the lives of those to whom we minister.

1) Model contentment with what you have.

Paul had needs that obviously needed to be met, especially now that he was under arrest, and the Philippian gift to him had indeed met the needs. But he was not as concerned with the gift as he was with the Philippians themselves. With regard to his needs, Paul had learned how to have much or how to have little. Each extreme has obvious temptations, as best articulated by Agur, the author of Proverbs 30:

Two things have a required of thee, deny me them not before I die: Remove far from me vanity and lies: give me neither poverty nor riches; feed me with food convenient [allotted portion] for me: Lest I be full, and deny thee, and say, Who is the LORD? or lest I be poor and steal, and take the name of my God in vain.

Doubtless many of us concur with Agur's sentiments: wealth (or the lack thereof) carries with it many temptations. Greed can look respectable, as one may appear to be a diligent worker. On the other end of the spectrum, those who are poor can resort to sinful activities in their quest to survive, for doing so seems justified. But Paul said that the secret to handling money well was clear: he could "do all things through Christ."

We are familiar with this verse since it is often quoted by athletes as a motivational mantra. The Golden State Warriors' Steph Curry writes it on every pair of his basketball shoes. And if Paul's words here referred to athletic victory it would be a hollow promise indeed. Most of us will never shoot NBA three pointers, or even do well in local pick-up games. Paul is saying he can do anything that the Lord would want him to do, regardless of the difficulty of it, through Christ. In fact, by Christ Paul could do what most of us fail to do: handle either little or much money well. Not that such is easy, for Paul confessed it had been a learning process for him. But it is possible.

2) Help others become good money managers.

Paul was not seeking a gift for the gift's sake. But he was seeking fruit to the Philippians account. There is a discussion on budgeting that is outside the scope of this message. But a few foundational principles should still be noted. First, each family unit should have a budget, with a regular plan for giving. Second, pastors should understand the basics of money and teach their people to be good money managers. Often a layman with expertise can be a great help. Those facts are clear.

The difficult part for budgeting comes when assigning a percentage for each individual budget category including giving. A large percentage of the budget for the normal family will be given to providing basic food, clothing, shelter, etc. But how much to give to ministry should also be a part of that budget. Traditionally churches have suggested believers give a tithe on their income (10% of the gross). A tithe may be a good place to begin, but it is not a New Testament command. Bruce Waltke offers the following helpful summary of New Testament teaching:

After Christ sends the Holy Spirit, however, his apostles drop the principle of tithing for a higher spiritual standard. God's people first give themselves to God (Rom. 12:1-2; 2 Cor. 8:5). Then they return material blessings to those who bring spiritual blessing (1 Cor. 9:6-18; Gal. 6:6) and give gifts to needy saints (Rom. 15:25-28; 1 Cor. 16:1-3; 2 Cor. 8:1-15; Gal. 6:10; Eph. 4:28). The principle now is: 'Whoever sows sparingly will also reap sparingly, and whoever sows generously will also reap generously' (2 Cor. 9:6; cf. Gal. 6:9). Christians are to do so eagerly, generously, and cheerfully, the amount depending on one's level of prosperity.[34]

That sentiment seemed well understood by the early church fathers, who thought a Christian should give more than that which was required by Mosaic Law.[35] One cannot help but feel they are correct. I would never wish to start micro managing anyone's finances. And all of us spend money to purchase items not necessary to our basic survival. But I would suggest that many of us should go beyond a tithe after prayerful consideration. Whenever money is spent, a value judgement has been made. The spender has decided that the money should be spent on _____ instead of having spent it on something else. What do our purchases reveal that we value the most? Do they reflect the ownership of the Lord and His concerns or our own desire to have nice possessions? Do we believe we can afford to spend $40,000 on a vehicle (not difficult to do in this day) when $20,000 would be perfectly adequate, but cannot sacrificially fund a ministry? A budget reflects priorities and giving should be a priority.

3) Focus on the true objective: ministry.

Paul's testimony later is that many other churches did nothing to support him. One imagines this neglect was discouraging. Paul already suffered greatly from persecution, whether verbal or physical in nature. Should he not at least have freedom from worry about his basic needs? In both Thessalonica and Corinth Paul worked. And it both cases his willingness to work was an important part of his evangelistic strategy. He was in both

---

[34] Bruce Waltke with Cathi Fredricks, *Genesis: A Commentary* (Grand Rapids, Mich.: Zondervan, 2001), 397.

[35] Richard Averbeck, "מַעֲשֵׂר," *New International Dictionary of Old Testament Theology and Exegesis*, 5 vols., ed. Willem VanGemeren (Grand Rapids, Mich.: Zondervan, 1997): 2:1054.

cities to minister and truly had the interests of others in mind. He worked rather than expecting financial remuneration. The Philippians, of course, had been a happy exception. They repeatedly showed concern for Paul, and Paul is careful to thank the Philippians for partnering in ministry. But even here his concern for ministry is evident. He assures them that their gift was pleasing to the Lord and was even above and beyond what he needed.

So those in ministry should follow Paul's example here: praise the Lord for those who support ministries, model contentment, help others become good money managers, and focus on ministry objectives. Based on the example of Paul and the subsequent response of the Philippian church, how should individual believers partner in ministry?

Believers in General

1) Have a consistent concern for ministry.

The Philippian letter marked the third time the church sent help to Paul. In a situation where no church had helped the apostle in the beginning, their consistency was all the more commendable. Of course, partnering in ministry always begins with one's own church. At the same time, there will doubtless be other worthy ministries that the church decides to fund. If we have a true concern for ministry, we will want to partner with them through financial support. You won't necessarily give to every worthy ministry, but you will partner with many while wishing you could help even more. At the very least a church should inquire of the missionaries it supports to see if their support level is adequate.

2) Sacrificially partner with those in ministry.

With the beatings, the imprisonments, the shipwrecks, and the overall hostility of Jews and Gentiles, ministry was very difficult for Paul. When the Philippians sent to meet his needs they had literally shared in Paul's affliction, removing a portion of the burden he carried and taking it on themselves. He no longer needed to worry about how he was to be fed while in prison. Paul confessed he had an abundance and had been filled, so the gift must have been generous. This testimony of Paul draws attention to the fact that when we do not manage our money well and do not give, we place an undue burden on anyone in vocational ministry. We refuse to sacrifice on behalf of those making great sacrifice.

The two principles are to have a consistent concern for ministry and sacrificially participate in it. It is a simple and easily understood set of directives, and yet we find that obedience is far more difficult in practice. Before we can correct that situation, however, we must understand why people behave as they do. All sin comes from the heart, of course, but how it manifests itself varies depending on life situation.

As Agur, those living in the modern United States find themselves prone to the same temptations. Money can dominate our thinking to a degree that it dictates our behavior in all sorts of ways. Perhaps no century in the history of the World has exhibited the variety of life circumstances as the United States has over the past 100 years. From the Roaring 20's, to the Depression, to World War II, to the postwar prosperity, to the era of the global economy, socio-economic change has been profound. And depending on when you grew up, you were likely subject to different influences from someone born as little as 10 years before or after you. It is important to understand that fact because deficiencies in our financial stewardship often align closely with the period of time during which we grew up.

Demographers generally recognize the following discernable groups in the United States:

- The Silent Generation (1925-45)
- Baby Boomers (1946-64)
- Gen X (1965-79)
- Millennials (1980-2000)
- Gen Z (2001-)36

The pastor of the church I attended during the early 1990s noted the differences in the way the generations viewed and handled money. At the time, the church consisted mostly of the Silent Generation and Baby Boomers (older Gen Xers were just entering adulthood). He observed that it was much easier to get the Silent Generation to volunteer their time

---

[36] Mark Vowels, "Millennials: Why the Next Generation Will Change the Way We Do Missions." Paper presented at National Leadership Conference, Central Seminary, Minneapolis, MN

than to give their money. Conversely, it was much easier to get the Boomers to give their money than their time.

It is not difficult to understand how the different outlooks developed. The Silent Generation lived through the Depression and World War II. During the Depression, unemployment was high. Since money was scarce, people hesitated to spend it. Once the United States entered World War II, however, unemployment ceased to be a problem. Every able-bodied man was needed for either the military or the defense industry, and women also entered the workforce in great numbers. But even though people were working, sacrifice was still a key principle. Consumer goods were now in short supply due to the war. It is easy to see why this generation tended to be more generous with time but less generous with money. They were very much used to spending little and saving much.

But then the war ended, and the world got busy rebuilding. With much of the rest of the world's industrial capacity destroyed, the United States quickly became the major supplier of manufactured goods. The joblessness of the depression followed by scarcity of the war years quickly gave way to prosperity and security (including generous retirements and health insurance). The change to the US economy was seismic. People now had money but tended to have less time as they began families and focused on personal goals.

Now, both the Silent Generation and the Boomers have obvious strengths: one is frugal and the other is generous. But taken to an extreme either one can frustrate ministry efforts. For the Silent Generation, it is good to save, but not good to hesitate to give when you can. For the Boomers, it is good to give, but not to sacrifice your involvement in ministry because you are so busy.

As the Boomer generation was succeeded by the remaining generations, the United States continued to change, leaving a somewhat different mark on each successive generation. The Gen Xers (1965-79) grew up in a world where every generation had more wealth than the previous one. They were used to a higher standard of living and believed they would inevitably have more wealth than their parents. But the rest of the world was catching up. Foreign competition intensified. Jobs began to depart for foreign countries; wages and benefits became stagnant, then decreased. The expectation of a life of wealth followed by a somewhat harsher reality produced a generation less prepared to manage money well. They felt that money was abundant and that getting more of it was not a particular problem. And it did create problems, especially since this was the first generation that grew up entirely during the age of ubiquitous television advertising. Generally speaking Gen Xers have the "most credit card debt of anyone—yet still spend more than anyone on non-essentials. ... [Are] woefully under-saved for retirement. ... [And their] overall debt load is the highest of any generation." [37] The problem for Gen Xers is that they may not be able to partner in ministry much at all. If you are in debt, you do not have money; furthermore, you are starting to run out of wage-earning years while inching ever closer to retirement.

Millennials and Gen Z, of course, have more time to adjust their financial habits. Each has some defining characteristics, but they are more similar to each other and even to Gen Xers than the preceding generations. Millennials "experience delayed adulthood or extended adolescence. They marry later, are financially dependent on their parents far longer, postpone embarking on a specific career and seem less concerned about financial stability than previous generations." [38] Gen Z is less optimistic and more risk averse, but still want things. [39] It seems they may not be as quick to foolishly take on debt as their parents and grandparents, but will not be content to live as sacrificially as the Silent Generation did. Both sets of characteristics carry challenges, especially as the generations stay dependent on parents longer while showing less interest in giving.

As argued above, handling money well can only be done in the Spirit's power. Doubtless some people will through their life situation naturally buck the trend. But the above survey should also sensitize us to where our blind spots are most likely to be. The early years in a person's life are formative. We will start to feel comfortable with certain attitudes and ways of living whether or not they are right simply through familiarity. People from the Silent Generation were known to stash money in

---

[37] Catey Hill, "All the ways Gen X is financially wrecked," Sept 12, 2018, Marketwatch.com, accessed 11/26/18.

[38] Mark Vowels, "Millennials: Why the Next Generation Will Change the Way We Do Missions."

[39] See Riley Griffin, "Move over, millennials: It's Gen Z's turn to kill industries," Aug. 7, 2018, https://www.msn.com/en-us/money/markets/move-over-millennials-it%e2%80%99s-gen-zs-turn-to-kill-industries/ar-BBLBeAd?li=BBnbfcN, accessed 8/24/18

mattresses, coffee tins, drawers, or any number of other "safe spots." And one can understand why. During the Depression when large numbers of banks failed a person could find themselves with no money. But nobody in Gen Z stashes cash around the house. Many do not even carry cash. Why bother when you can use your Apple Pay and avoid fumbling through a wallet looking for paper dollars?

We must all be self-critical and ask ourselves: "Is my money management a result of conformity to the Lord's goals or am I being controlled by various cultural influences. As the above survey shows, regardless of when you grew up, your environment may influence you to view money wrongly. To the degree that a cultural trend wrongly influences the way I view supporting ministry it must be identified and corrected by scriptural teaching. Then, though handling my money may prove difficult, I will have to learn to do it "through Christ who strengthens me."

Conclusion: What does the Lord think about a commitment to give?

If I learn how God expects me to handle money and learn to handle it well by the Lord's power, what will He think about it? When people sacrificially partner in ministry, it is a pleasing sacrifice in the Lord's view (18). And God promises that He will supply your needs. Of course, we must be careful how we define needs, for often we think we need things better described as "wants." But whatever your needs are, Paul is careful to note that God's ability to apply them is unlimited. His provision is not that of a human with finite resources but is according to riches in glory. Human limits on earth do not operate in heaven.

If we do not manage our money well, Christ's words in Luke 16:8-13 will apply to us:

> And the lord [the master of the unjust steward] commended the unjust steward, because he had done wisely: for the children of this world are in their generation wiser than the children of light. And I say unto you, Make to yourselves friends of the mammon of unrighteousness; that, when ye fail, they may receive you into everlasting habitations. He that is faithful in that which is least is faithful also in much: and he that is unjust in the least is unjust also in much. If therefore ye have not been faithful in the unrighteous mammon, who will commit to your trust the true riches? And if ye have not been faithful in that which is another man's, who shall give you that which is your own? No servant can

serve two masters: for either he will hate the one, and love the other; or else he will hold to the one, and despise the other. Ye cannot serve God and mammon.

Are you managing your money well, looking to the day when you will leave it all behind and be with the Lord and his people—the very people that your support of ministry helped to reach and disciple? Or are you allowing various cultural influences—whatever form they take—to hinder your support for ministry.

MARANATHA BAPTIST BIBLE INSTITUTE

A Passion for BIBLE

- Bible and Church Ministries Certificate
- College Campus Experience
- Affordable Pricing
- Financial Aid Available

Prepare for a lifetime of local church service!

Visit **mbu.edu/mbbi** or talk with us
at **800.622.2947** today to learn more.

MARANATHA BAPTIST SEMINARY

A Passion for **LOCAL CHURCH**

- Baptist & Dispensational
- Residential & Online Programs
- Afforadable Tuition

Any Class. Anywhere. On your time.

Visit **mbu.edu/seminary** or talk with us at **920.206.2324** today to learn more.

MASTER OF ORGANIZATIONAL LEADERSHIP

A Passion to LEAD

- Add Value to Your Organization
- Build Leadership Skills
- Complete Entirely Online

Increase your knowledge of the business dynamics in organizations of all sizes!

Biblical. Flexible. Engaging.
Visit **mbu.edu/grad** or talk with us
at **800.622.2947** today to learn more.

MASTER OF EDUCATION IN TEACHING AND LEADING

A Passion to **TEACH**

- Entirely Online
- Regionally Accredited
- Cost Effective

Continue your ministry while advancing your education!

MARANATHA
BAPTIST UNIVERSITY

Biblical. Flexible. Engaging.
Visit **mbu.edu/grad** or talk with us
at **800.622.2947** today to learn more.

Made in the USA
Middletown, DE
10 June 2021

41774143R00060